Connect with Taquetta and KSM at <u>kingdomshifters.com</u> or via Facebook. For more information regarding Bishop Jackie Green at <u>Jgmenternational.org</u>.

I0150026

Taquetta's Table of Contents

Book Synopsis

"FEASTING IN HIS PRESENCE" is
for ANYONE who desires to soak, heal and be
transformed in heaven's miracle working power,
while deepening their relationship with Jesus.
Receive biblical insight on the difference between
witchcraft versus soaking prayer, dangers of yoga,
relinquishing blockages to soaking prayer,
benefits of soaking, and how to soak. Expand
your knowledge and experiences regarding the
power of resting in the Lord's presence and
strengthening your intimate relationship with
him, as he makes your private communion public
such that you live healed and whole in your mind,
body, soul, generations, ministry, and lifestyle.

Feasting In His Presence

TaquettaBaker@Kingdomshifters.com

(Website) Kingdomshifters.com

Connect with Taquetta via Facebook or Youtube
Copyright 2011 – Kingdom Shifters Ministries

Taquetta's Bio

Taquetta Baker is the founder of Kingdom Shifters Ministries (KSM). She has authored fourteen books and two decree CD's. Taquetta has a Master's Degree in Community Counseling with an emphasis on Marriage, Children and Family Counseling, a Bachelor's Degree in Psychology and Associates Degree in Business Administration. In addition, Taquetta has a Therapon Belief Therapist Certification from Therapon Institute and has 22 years of professional and Christian Counseling experience.

Taquetta is also gifted at empowering and assisting people with launching ministries, businesses and books and provides mentoring, counseling and vision casting through Kingdom Shifters Kingdom Wellness Program. Taquetta serves on the Board of Directors for New Day Community Ministries, Inc. of Muncie, IN. In October 2008, Taquetta graduated from the Eagles Dance Institute under Dr. Pamela Hardy and received her license in liturgical dance. Before launching into her own ministry, Taquetta served at her previous church for 12 years. She was a prophet, pioneer and leader of Shekinah Expressions Dance Ministry, teacher, member of the presbytery board, and overseer of the Altar Workers Ministry. Taquetta receives mentoring and ministry covering from Bishop Jackie Green, Founder of JGM-National PrayerLife Institute (Phoenix, AZ), and was ordained as an Apostle on June 7, 2014.

Taquetta flows through the wells of warfare and worship and mantles an apostolic mandate of judging and establishing God's kingdom in people, ministries, communities, and regions. Taquetta travels in foreign missions and throughout the United States. She has mentored and established dance, altar workers, deliverance, and prophetic ministries. Taquetta ministers in the areas of fine arts, all manners of prayer, fivefold ministry, deliverance, healing, miracles, atmospheric worship, and empowers and train people in their destiny and life's vision.

Forward

I was first introduced to soaking while visiting Apostle Baker's home about ten years ago. I had just gotten off the road from a four hour trip from Chicago, Illinois to Muncie, Indiana. I was tired, hungry and anxious to lay down and relax. When I entered Apostle Baker's home I noticed a shift in the atmosphere from my car to her foyer. Where I was tired, weary and irritable, I began to instantaneously feel refreshed and at peace. The presence of God was so strong in her house that it was palpable. As soft music played throughout the house, I asked Apostle Baker, what was going on in her home that the presence of God was so strong. She responded that she had been soaking. I had never heard of soaking before and inquired more. That weekend Apostle Baker began to explain soaking and demonstrate soaking for me. Since then, my spiritual life has not been the same. Soaking is a spiritual discipline I practice everyday and has brought me closer to God.

Apostle Baker is a woman of integrity who loves basking in the presence of God. The presence of God is within her and envelopes her. She is an amazingly strong force in the army of God who is wise beyond her years. Apostle Baker is ready to minister in season and out because of the many hours she spends in the presence of God studying, praying, worshiping, in warfare and soaking.

Because of Apostle Baker's intimate relationship with God, I was excited to hear she had written *Feasting in His Presence Tools for Soaking and Deepening Your Kingdom Relationship with Jesus* to share the spiritual discipline of soaking with others. Apostle Baker has poured her heart and soul into this book. She gives us a solid foundation of what soaking is and how we can use it effectively in our lives. Apostle Baker skillfully combines her knowledge of the Bible, soaking and counseling into this account. The book is also a fine teaching resource. I have found it to be one of the most thorough writings on soaking that I plan to use in workshops and life coaching sessions.

I found the sections of the book featuring activations and journaling exercises to be most beneficial and her poetry inspiring. Even a new comer to soaking can catch on quickly to this spiritual practice and see results quickly.

Feasting in His Presence Tools for Soaking and Deepening Your Kingdom Relationship with Jesus is an excellent book that will surely transform and deepen the spiritual life of a believer. May your heart, mind, soul and spirit be open and ready to be blessed as you read the coming pages.

Rev. Ayanna Garrett, MDIV, M.Ed in Community Counseling
Living Water Community Church, Bolingbrook, IL

Forward

I call **Feasting In His Presence** the lifestyle changer and the lifestyle cultivator. When you partake of it, your desire for a deeper lifestyle immersed in Jesus and a new hunger to mature in greater relationship with the Lord will be birthed in you. When God calls you to a new place and level of relationship with Him, this is a go to book that will help guide you as you form fresh foundation in God and instill new practices in your daily life. The applications throughout the book lead you as you cultivate yourself in feasting in Jesus while also bringing healing and deliverance as it works in you. Soaking will change your life, as it is the place where you can completely move out of the way and let God work, speak, move, fill, heal, deliver, seal, consume, overtake and so many others things. Soaking is the place where you can just fall into the arms of God and sink into the heart of the Father as you totally surrender, rest and let go of all worry and cares inside of him. Soaking is one of the most underrated and misunderstood lifestyle practices that God has given us. I believe it is for this reason that we experience excessive tiredness, weariness, stress, heaviness, burnout, depression and more. We live our lives constantly wanting to do, never leaving any room for God to do for us which he so desires to do. He loves us and we are his children. God reminds us frequently throughout his word that there is rest for us, that we are to cast our burdens on him, that our peace is in him. He even goes as far as to warn us not to miss out on our rest, Hebrews 4:10-11 in the amplified version says, For the one who has once entered His rest has also rested from [the weariness and pain of] his [human] labors, just as God rested from [those labors uniquely] His own. Let us therefore make every effort to enter that rest [of God, to know and experience it for ourselves], so that no one will fall by *following* the same example of disobedience [as those who died in the wilderness]. God wants us to rest and this book will guide you in taking time to rest daily by soaking in God and making soaking a part of your lifestyle.

The author takes the time to discuss and examine spirits and behaviors that can operate as hindrances to soaking in our lives. This is important for us to know such that the enemy does not steal the treasures that God has stored for us through soaking. Before reading this book, I had never read insight on the spirit of drama at this depth that dissected how it operates and why. Being delivered from participating in, provoking and being a victim of drama is imperative. This book takes the deliverance another step further by applying the concept of soaking. Instead of receiving satisfaction from the ecstasy the drama produces, it transforms the life of the person to embody healthy practices while snuffing out the power and need for drama. True fulfillment, balance, wholeness, peace, tranquility, deeper relationship with God and healthy interactions with people are some of the fruits formed as soaking produces in your life.

I love how the book breaks down the practice and foundational roots of yoga and makes precise distinctions between it and soaking. The distinctions will help shift people from bondage they may unknowingly be entangled in, while bringing biblical revelation about soaking. Scriptures on meditation, communing with God, and resting in God are listed throughout the book to help the reader understand the concept of soaking, its use and necessity, and how God designed it as a blessing of intimacy in relationship with him. Witchcraft and yoga seek to tap into this place of peace, tranquility and fulfillment through illegal supernatural activity and the worship of the idol gods to which it draws its power. The author breaks these operations down discussing the worship of Hindu religions, illegal supernatural experiences such as astral projection, and witchcraft operations that you can become subject to through yoga. The biblical insight given on the deceptive and demonic nature of yoga will fill the reader with knowledge and enlighten them to the truth.

The fruit of this book will be immediately evident as you feast in God's presence and apply the concept of soaking to your life. Through the author, God has created a book that will change and shape lives, help to cultivate deeper relationships with the Lord, and expose hidden demonic practices that seek to mimic what can only be produced authentically through God. Let the revelation and power of this book be limitless in the lives of every person that feasts upon it!

Minister Nina Cook

Apostle Taquetta's Armor-bearer and Spiritual Daughter

BASKING IN HIS PRESENCE!

Basking in Your glory! Basking in Your grace!
Serenading in Your harmonious presence that has filled my holy
place.

Your presence is like sweet perfume masquerading Your tender
touch; basking in Your awesome presence, experiencing the
essence of your anointed hush.

Your warm, comforting affection, envelopes me in Your glorious,
miraculous light. I am basking in Your glory…Your
presence….Heavenly slain….just me and my true Christ.

Basking in Your adoration…A favor that is simply too much. In
the aroma of Your fragrance, I feel Your sweet approbation
proving me worthy to experience Your unconditional love.

Being purified in Your glory…Your presence is where I long to
live. Basking in Your glory! Basking in Your grace! Serenading
in Your harmonious presence that has filled my holy place!

BASKING IN YOUR PRESENCE!
By: TAQUETTA BAKER

KINGDOM COMMUNING

Since the beginning of mankind, God desired to commune with man. As much as it is a blessing to us, it is also a treat and a pleasure for God.

> *Genesis 3:8-11 And they heard the voice of the LORD God walking in the garden in the cool of the day: and Adam and his wife hid themselves from the presence of the LORD God amongst the trees of the garden. And the LORD God called unto Adam, and said unto him, Where [art] thou? And he said, I heard thy voice in the garden, and I was afraid, because I [was] naked; and I hid myself. And he said, Who told thee that thou [wast] naked? Hast thou eaten of the tree, whereof I commanded thee that thou shouldest not eat?*

The word says that the voice of the Lord was walking in the garden in the cool of the day. We know that when taking a walk in the cool of the day, it is usually to enjoy the breeze, to release the day, and to fellowship with others we may be taking a walk with. God was letting it be known that he desired to commune with Adam. He was coming to fellowship with him and to enjoy the cool of the day with him.

The Hebrew word for *Cool* is *Ruwach* and means:
1. wind, breath, mind, spirit
2. of heaven, breath of air, heaven
3. spirit (as that which breathes quickly in animation or agitation)
4. spirit, animation, vivacity, vigor, courage
5. prophetic spirit, as inspiring ecstatic state of prophecy
6. as gift, preserved by God, God's spirit, departing at death, disembodied being
7. spirit (as seat of emotion), desire, as seat or organ of mental acts,

8. rarely of the will, as seat especially of moral character
9. Spirit of God, the third person of the triune God, the Holy Spirit, coequal, coeternal with the Father and the Son
10. imparting warlike energy and executive and administrative power
11. as endowing men with various gifts, as energy of life
12. as manifest in the Shekinah glory

Ruwach is the same Hebrew word for the *Holy Spirit* or *wind of God.* God was not only desiring to fellowship with Adam, he made sure it was beautiful by manifesting his presence within the cool of the day where Adam could enjoy being in his midst and feasting of his pleasures.

A few of Merriam Webster's Online definitions of *Cool* is:
1. free from tensions or violence
2. very good, excellent
3. fashionable
4. relief from heat
5. calm, composed

God desired to relax with Adam, or as the youngsters say, "chill with him." We see however, as the story reads that though God had forbidden Adam and Eve to eat from the tree of good and evil, they gave in to the trick of the serpent and put shame between them and God.

> **Verse 10-12** *And the LORD God called unto Adam, and said unto him, Where [art] thou? And he said, I heard thy voice in the garden, and I was afraid, because I [was] naked; and I hid myself. And he said, Who told thee that thou [wast] naked? Hast thou eaten of the tree, whereof I commanded thee that thou shouldest not eat? And the man said, The woman whom thou gavest [to be] with me, she gave me of the tree, and I did eat.*

Verse 22-24 And the LORD God said, Behold, the man is become as one of us, to know good and evil: and now, lest he put forth his hand, and take also of the tree of life, and eat, and live for ever: Therefore the LORD God sent him forth from the garden of Eden, to till the ground from whence he was taken. So he drove out the man; and he placed at the east of the garden of Eden Cherubims, and a flaming sword which turned every way, to keep the way of the tree of life.

It was disobedience and sin that separated God and Adam from their daily communion. Yet, we see all throughout God's word that this is still his desire. He wrapped himself in flesh just so he could restore communion with us, and thus again, have those daily walks of fellowship.

FEASTING JESUS

Feed me from your gleaming presence Jesus!
Evade my atmosphere with the aroma of your fragrant presence.
Drench me from the healing waters of your glory rain.
My existence becoming a venture of oneness with your
astonishing heavens.

Feasting at the altar of worship.
Saturated in your irrevocable name.
Glory waters bubbling over.
Renewed wine...fresh life...a joy I cannot contain.

Savoring! Grubbing! Fulfilling provision directly from you.
My sphere is partaking of your Spirit and truth.
As when you douse, everything gets drenched...a deluge of
eternal plunging...holy satisfaction...that cannot be stifle or
quenched.

You are my life, the air I breathe.
You are my food...my water source, my ahhhh after a drink.
A cultivated lifestyle of covenant relationship, living here inside
the feast...paving the way for generational inheritance, kingly
legacy of sons & daughters...feasting from your wondrous bliss.

Feasting Jesus!

Because God desires communion with us, we too should
desire to bask in his presence and feast of his goodness.

> **Psalms 16:11** *Thou wilt show me the path of life: in thy*
> *presence is fullness of joy; at thy right hand there are*
> *pleasures for evermore.*

Fullness is *Soba* in the Hebrew and means:
1. fullness
2. satiety

3. abundance

<u>Merriam Webster's Online Dictionary defines *Fullness* as:</u>
1. the quality or state of being full, in the fullness of time, at some point, eventually
2. completely filled; containing all that can be held; filled to utmost capacity
3. complete; entire; maximum, of the maximum size, amount, extent, volume, etc.
4. (of garments, drapery, etc.) wide, ample, or having ample folds
5. abundant; well-supplied, filled or rounded out
6. the highest or fullest state, condition, or degree

God's presence is where we get direction and satisfaction. It is in his presence that we receive abundance, completion, and overflow from anything the world is lacking.

> *Psalms 34:8-10 (The Amplified Version) O taste and see that the Lord [our God] is good! Blessed (happy, fortunate, to be envied) is the man who trusts and takes refuge in Him. O fear the Lord, you His saints [revere and worship Him]! For there is no want to those who truly revere and worship Him with godly fear. The young lions lack food and suffer hunger, but they who seek (inquire of and require) the Lord [by right of their need and on the authority of His Word], none of them shall lack any beneficial thing.*

> *(The Message Version) Open your mouth and taste, open your eyes and see – how good God is Blessed are you who run to him. Worship God if you want the best; worship opens doors to all his goodness. Young lions on the prowl get hungry, but God-seekers are full of God.*

David began this verse by saying, "*O taste.*" What David was experiencing was complete satisfaction. It was

obvious it was good to his soul because he was saying,
"OOOOOOOOOOOOOOOO taste." This kind of tasting is not
just a feeling, but David was tasting and experiencing the
flavor of God. He was coming into a divine understanding
and knowledge of the benefits of being lost inside God's
presence. That word taste is *Ta am* and means to "*taste,
perceive, eat.*" David was not just resting inside God's
presence, he was feasting on it, and what he was
experiencing was giving him a revelation of the goodness
of God.

Merriam Webster's Online dictionary defines *Taste* as:
1. to try or test the flavor or quality of (something) by
   taking some into the mouth
2. to eat or drink a little of, to eat or drink
3. to perceive or distinguish the flavor of
4. to have or get experience, especially a slight experience
5. to perceive in any way, to enjoy or appreciate
6. examine by touch; feel, to test or try
7. to try the flavor or quality of something
8. to have experience of something, however limited or
   slight
9. to have a particular flavor, to smack or savor
10. the sense by which the flavor or savor of things is
    perceived when they are brought into contact with the
    tongue
11. the sensation or quality as perceived by this sense;
    flavor
12. a small quantity tasted; a morsel, bit, or sip
13. a relish, liking, or partiality for something
14. the sense of what is fitting, harmonious, or beautiful;
    the perception and enjoyment of what constitutes
    excellence in the fine arts, literature, fashion, etc.

I know you are probably saying, "Why did she list all
those definitions?" But if you read each of them then I

know just like David, it placed an "OOOOOOOO" in your Spirit to want to taste the goodness of the Lord. I am a lover of the word so please admonish me while I share a few scriptures in different versions regarding drinking and feasting Jesus.

Matthew 26:26-28 *And as they were eating, Jesus took bread, and blessed it, and brake it, and gave it to the disciples, and said, Take, eat: this is my body. And he took the cup, and gave thanks, and gave it to them, saying, Drink ye all of it; for this is my blood of the new testament, which is shed for many for the remission of sins. But I say unto you, I will not drink henceforth of this fruit of the vine, until that day when I drink it new with you in my Father's kingdom.*

(The Amplified Version) Now as they were eating, Jesus took bread and, praising God, gave thanks and asked Him to bless it to their use, and when He had broken it, He gave it to the disciples and said, Take, eat; this is My body. And He took a cup, and when He had given thanks, He gave it to them, saying, Drink of it, all of you; for this is My blood of the new covenant, which ratifies the agreement and] is being poured out for many for the forgiveness of sins. I say to you, I shall not drink again of this fruit of the vine until that day when I drink it with you new and of superior quality in My Father's kingdom.

(Good News Translation) While they were eating, Jesus took a piece of bread, gave a prayer of thanks, broke it, and gave it to his disciples. "Take and eat it," he said; "this is my body." Then he took a cup, gave thanks to God, and gave it to them. "Drink it, all of you," he said; "this is my blood, which seals God's covenant, my blood poured out for many for the forgiveness of sins. I tell you, I will never again drink this wine until the day I drink the new wine with you in my Father's Kingdom.

(The Message Version) During the meal, Jesus took and blessed the bread, broke it, and gave it to his disciples: Take, eat. This is my body. Taking the cup and thanking God, he gave it to them: Drink this, all of you. This is my blood, God's new covenant poured out for many people for the forgiveness of sins. "I'll not be drinking wine from this cup again until that new day when I'll drink with you in the kingdom of my Father."

Luke 22:18-20 *For I say unto you, I will not drink of the fruit of the vine, until the kingdom of God shall come. And he took bread, and gave thanks, and brake it, and gave unto them, saying, This is my body which is given for you: this do in remembrance of me. 20 Likewise also the cup after supper, saying, this cup is the new testament in my blood, which is shed for you.*

(The Message Version) Taking bread, he blessed it, broke it, and gave it to them, saying, "This is my body, given for you. Eat it in my memory." He did the same with the cup after supper, saying, "This cup is the new covenant written in my blood, blood poured out for you.

1Corinthians 11:24:33 *And when he had given thanks, he brake it, and said, Take, eat: this is my body, which is broken for you: this do in remembrance of me. After the same manner also he took the cup, when he had supped, saying, this cup is the new testament in my blood: this do ye, as oft as ye drink it, in remembrance of me. For as often as ye eat this bread, and drink this cup, ye do shew the Lord's death till he come*

(The Message Version) Having given thanks, he broke it and said, this is my body, broken for you. Do this to remember me. After supper, he did the same thing with the cup: This cup is my blood, my new covenant with you. Each time you drink this cup, remember me. What you must solemnly realize is that every time you eat this bread and every time you drink this cup, you reenact in your words and actions the death of the

Master. You will be drawn back to this meal again and again until the Master returns. You must never let familiarity breed contempt.

I am praying that as you read those passages of scriptures, you heard Jesus wooing you to drink and eat of his presence. Often when we consider these scriptures, we think taking communion and this is indeed the case, but if you explore the scriptures further, you will discern that Jesus was speaking of his literal body and not just an act of partaking of wine and bread. Even when Jesus was explaining eating the bread and the wine in remembrance of him, he was communing with the disciples. He was fellowshipping with them and sharing how he desired further fellowship and for them to spend time remembering him and the things he did for them even after his death. I believe this was because Jesus knew he was leaving the Holy Spirit to comfort the disciples and he wanted to set the stage for them further communing with his presence even though he would no longer be with them in the flesh.

> **John 14:16** *And I will pray the Father, and he shall give you another Comforter, that he may abide with you for ever.*
>
> **Verse 26** *But the Comforter, [which is] the Holy Ghost, whom the Father will send in my name, he shall teach you all things, and bring all things to your remembrance, whatsoever I have said unto you.*
>
> **John 15:26-27** *But when the Comforter is come, whom I will send unto you from the Father, [even] the Spirit of truth, which proceedeth from the Father, he shall testify of me: And ye also shall bear witness, because ye have been with me from the beginning.*

Comforter is in the Greek is *Paraklētos* and means:

1. summoned, called to one's side, esp. called to one's aid
2. one who pleads another's cause before a judge, a pleader, counsel for defense, legal assistant, an advocate
3. one who pleads another's cause with one, an intercessor
4. of Christ in his exaltation at God's right hand, pleading with God the Father for the pardon of our sins
5. in the widest sense, a helper, aider, assistant
6. of the Holy Spirit destined to take the place of Christ with the apostles (after his ascension to the Father), to lead them to a deeper knowledge of the gospel truth, and give them divine strength needed to enable them to undergo trials and persecutions on behalf of the divine kingdom

Jesus said he was sending a Comforter to testify of him and that the disciples should be able to bear witness with the Comforter, because they have been with him since the beginning of his ministry. Have you ever had a stranger comfort you when you are going through a trial? I watch a lot of doctor shows and many doctors look so uncomfortable when they comfort a grieving patient. Comforting patients is part of their job and they do not want to seem inconsiderate, but because there is no relationship, it can make for a very awkward and uncomfortable experience. Yet when someone you know comforts you, someone you have a relationship with, it is a very safe, relaxing and soothing experience. The only way to be truly comforted is through communion and Jesus sent his presence, the ultimate Comforter, to commune and journey daily with the disciples. This was for the purposes of continuing the relationship that began in the garden when God walked with Adam in the cool of the day.

The Comforter was sent to teach which means he was sent to guide the path of our lives, and bring us into the fullness of the pleasures of God. This requires us spending time with God and basking in his presence. It thus requires us to feast in the presence of Jesus.

Feasting Jesus Activation:
1. What are your thoughts on being able to spiritually feast on the presence and goodness of Jesus?
2. What are your thoughts on being able to spiritually drink and eat of his saving blood and body?
3. Spend time spiritually drinking and eating the saving blood and body of Jesus Christ. Practice this for a week for at least five minutes at a time. Journal your experiences.
4. Spend time meditating on the goodness of Jesus and soaking in his goodness.
   a. Focus on what he has done for you and then absorb the fruit and blessing of what he has done.
   b. Then spend time focusing on what he has promised he would do. Absorb the wealth of his goodness and promises towards you while soaking.
   c. Spend time letting God know your desires. Ask him to reveal how he feels about your desires. Cleanse out any desires that are not his will for your life, while soaking in the expectation that he will fulfill your desires that align with his word and purpose for your life.
   d. Take feasting goodness soaks at least once a week to rejuvenate yourself in the goodness of the Lord.
5. What is your relationship with the Holy Spirit?
6. Spend time asking the Holy Spirit to comfort you. Practice this for a week for at least 15 minutes at a time. Journal your experiences.

SOAKING! GULPING JESUS

One great attribute about God is if we pursue him, we will find him.

James 4:8 *Draw near to God, and He will draw near to you.*

Proverbs 8:21 *I love them that love me; and those that seek me early shall find me.*

Jeremiah 29:13 *And ye shall seek me, and find [me], when ye shall search for me with all your heart.*

Hosea 5:15 *I will go [and] return to my place, till they acknowledge their offence, and seek my face: in their affliction they will seek me early.*

Isaiah 51:1 *Hearken to me, ye that follow after righteousness, ye that seek the LORD: look unto the rock [whence] ye are hewn, and to the hole of the pit [whence] ye are digged.*

Luke 11:9 *And I say unto you, Ask, and it shall be given you; seek, and ye shall find; knock, and it shall be opened unto you.*

Revelation 3:20 *Behold, I stand at the door, and knock: if any man hear my voice, and open the door, I will come in to him, and will sup with him, and he with me.*

God has made it clear that if we draw nigh unto him, he will be right there with open arms. Though I only made references here, there are a lot of scriptures that speak of seeking God early. Often we equate this to praying early in the morning. I personally enjoy starting my day off basking in what I call "morning glory," yet I do not feel that these scriptures are just speaking of time, as no matter what time we pray, God is ready and willing to commune with us. I therefore, believe these scriptures are speaking of:

> Seeking him before the enemy begins to cause havoc in our lives
> Seeking him before we make decisions
> Seeking him to lead the way in our journey
> Seeking him for comfort, encouragement and support
> Seeking him even before we need healing, as if our bodies are in constant communion with him then the less entrance the enemy has to afflict us

That word early is *Shachar* and means *"early or diligently."* I believe God is speaking of us having a consistent intimate pursuit of communing and building our relationship with him. This puts us on the offense and gives us an edge against anything that would occur in our lives.

Seeking Jesus Activation:
1. For seven days look for Jesus everywhere as you go throughout your day.
2. Ask Jesus to show himself as you are in the mall, at work, driving in the car, gazing in the sky, at church, people watching, engaging people, during situations, etc.
3. Seek to make yourself keenly aware that Jesus is everywhere.
4. Ask Jesus to heighten your discernment so you will know when he is and is not present.
5. When in prayer, ask God to reveal himself and seek to see him through how he is revealing himself. Do not rely on what you know or what you are used to experiencing with him. Focus on relaxing in his presence and allowing him to reveal himself to you.
6. Spend five minutes for the next 30 days telling God how hungry you are for him and how you desire to

experience him. Then wait five minutes to see how he responds to you.

7. Journal your experiences and use your revelation to further increase your hunger for more of him.

BENEFITS TO SOAKING & FEASTING

There are great benefits to soaking and feasting Jesus. Soaking:

- ❖ Builds a greater relationship with the Lord and his presence. Soaking is one of the greatest tools for drawing closer to Jesus and feasting on the pleasures of his presence.
- ❖ Changes your likeness to the character, nature, and essence of God.
- ❖ Teaches you how to surrender to the Holy Spirit, where you are guided by the Holy Spirit and not flesh, emotions, demons, or the world.
- ❖ Teaches you how to surrender to the will, purpose, and presence of God.
- ❖ Increases your ability to trust in the Lord and journey in unwavering faith in him.
- ❖ Fine tunes your senses and discernment; gives you a keener ear to God's voice, heart, and will.
- ❖ Teaches you the voice of God and provides an avenue to build trust where he will share his heart with you.
- ❖ Teaches you how to discern between good and evil; the Godly and the ungodly, and provides wisdom regarding judging and establishing judgment in the earth.
- ❖ Positions you to have divine dreams and visions that provide answers and strategies to problems and situations and yields future insight.
- ❖ Provides answers and strategies concerning problematic situations.
- ❖ Teaches you how to embrace and operate in the supernatural.
- ❖ Teaches you how to fulfill ministry tasks in spiritual realms.
- ❖ Refreshes and revives the mind, body, and spirit.

- ❖ Cleanses the sins and wounded areas of the soul, body, mind, and emotions.
- ❖ Brings breakthrough in areas where deliverance, healing, affliction, and sin has been difficult; reveals roots to sicknesses and afflictions and swallows up any legality of the enemy.
- ❖ Combats heaviness and releases burdens back to Jesus.
- ❖ Releases greater power and authority in your giftings and ministry, such that miracles, signs and wonders manifest.
- ❖ Teaches patience and obedience in waiting on God to speak and the manifestation of his will; teaches you how to wait in the will and strength of God, and empowers you until God's timing unfolds for that which you are waiting on.
- ❖ Releases information, strategies, and/or visions concerning God's destiny and will for your life; heals areas where your destiny has been altered, tainted, aborted, etc.
- ❖ Provides a refuge during challenging seasons; teaching you how to rest and trust God in seasons where he is silent and in general.
- ❖ Teaches and brings comfort in walking in obedience and unwavering faith; teaches you how to surrender totally to the presence and will of the Lord.
- ❖ Releases comfort, encouragement, refreshment, confirmation, conviction, etc., where needed.
- ❖ Provides an avenue for God to share how he feels about you and you to share your feelings and love for God; great way to build your love language for God and people in general.
- ❖ Teaches Godly communication skills and sets a pattern and standard for the attributes of a Godly relationship that demonstrates God's unconditional love and compassion.
- ❖ Matures you and provides a continual desire to elevate in your walk with the Lord.

- ❖ Makes you a glory carrier, as the more you gulp Jesus, the more you exude his image, his presence, and the ability to manifest his heavenly attributes with miracles, signs and wonders following.
- ❖ Creates a greater atmosphere for God's presence to dwell.
- ❖ Keeps you constantly connected and aligned with God and his presence.

LONGING FOR YOU!

The valley of my soul thirst for an outpouring of you.
A refreshing that can only manifest from your heavenly dew.

Mists so passionate they serenade the atmosphere.
Taking me away to a distant place, separating me from worldly
heartaches and fleshly hemispheres.

Quenching my dry heave soaking my waterless soul.
Rain down my Lord...let your love flow.

For it is you that I long for; the pleasures of your truth.
Spirit to Spirit connection, breathe into my soul anew.

And in my sob, a yearning plea, I hear God reply, "My gaze has
never left you, my beloved...my bride...I see tears of your soul
wailing out to me in a hollow cry."

"I am sending my drenching to replenish your joy, set your
nature free..."
"Releasing the humidity of my fragrance, therapeutically
vaporizing all of you with all of me..."

"For I too long to hear your praises, the ministering of My
Name."
"The intensity of your heartbeat...lets renew our love again."

And so we meet in the secret place...the bride and her king.
Longings fulfilled through a spiritual union of a hart that
panteth after the water brook, so my soul panteth after thee.

Longing For You!
By: Taquetta Baker

.

VAIN VERSUS HEALTHY IMAGINATION

SAY THIS WITH ME! *The bible tells us not to have vain or evil imagination. It does not condemn having or using our imagination.*

> **2Corinthians 10:4-6** *(For the weapons of our warfare are not carnal, but mighty through God to the pulling down of strong holds). Casting down imaginations, and every high thing that exalteth itself against the knowledge of God, and bringing into captivity every thought to the obedience of Christ; And having in a readiness to revenge all disobedience, when your obedience is fulfilled.*

> **(The Amplified Version)** *For the weapons of our warfare are not physical [weapons of flesh and blood], but they are mighty before God for the overthrow and destruction of strongholds, [Inasmuch as we] refute arguments and theories and reasonings and every proud and lofty thing that sets itself up against the [true] knowledge of God; and we lead every thought and purpose away captive into the obedience of Christ (the Messiah, the Anointed One). Being in readiness to punish every [insubordinate for his] disobedience, when your own submission and obedience [as a church] are fully secured and complete.*

Vain or evil imaginations become high places in our perceptions and lives, thus exalting themselves above God's lordship, commands, laws, word, will and purpose for our lives. Nothing should be greater than God. Usually when a belief, system, person, or thing has become greater than God, its existence began in our imagination. But this does not mean our imagination is bad. This just means we have contemplated and feasted on the wrong thing and the essence of our focus has become lord of our lives.

Philippians 4:8 states the following: *Finally, brethren, whatsoever things are true, whatsoever things [are] honest, whatsoever things [are] just, whatsoever things [are] pure, whatsoever things [are] lovely, whatsoever things [are] of good report; if [there be] any virtue, and if [there be] any praise, think on these things.*

Colossians 3:2 - *Set your affection on things above, not on things on the earth.*

Proverbs 4:23 - *Keep thy heart with all diligence; for out of it [are] the issues of life.*

Vain or evil imaginations are not the fruit, character or nature of God. When we have a vain or evil thought, we should immediately cast it down and continue doing so until it has surrendered under the Lordship of God and his word. To cast down means to destroy or demolish. That means it must be done with violence and force. It is not something to be taken lightly as a vain or evil imagination is seeking to take charge of you. You must continually be at war with vain and evil imaginations, such that they do not become your truth.

James 4:7 *Submit yourselves therefore to God. Resist the devil, and he will flee from you.*

1Peter 5:8 *Be sober, be vigilant; because your adversary the devil, as a roaring lion, walketh about, seeking whom he may devour.*

Hebrews 5:14 *But strong meat belongeth to them that are of full age, even those who by reason of use have their senses exercised to discern both good and evil.*

You cast down a vain or evil imagination by:
• Starving it – giving it no room when it initially forms

- Immediately crucifying it with the word, truth, and will of God – falling out of agreement with it and every way it is striving to be truth in your life
- Beating it down with the word of God – applying scriptures to it that refute and destroy its power over your life
- Not feeding your mind and appetite with vain and evil things (example: TV shows, social media and internet filth, ungodly or unhealthy conversations, demonic or worldly music)
- Maturing in God and his word so you can discern good from evil
- Refusing to become desensitized to pride, evil, sin, and worldliness
- Remaining offensive and ready to refute everything that is not of God

If we think on vainness and evil too long, we SHIFT into setting our affections in pursuit of it. Once we have partaken of it, we have awakened a desire for it within our will and flesh. If we continue to feed these imaginations, they become treasures of our heart and ideas, while causing issues and challenges in our lives and situations.

> *Ephesians 1:17-18* *That the God of our LORD Jesus Christ, the Father of glory, may give unto you the spirit of wisdom and revelation in the knowledge of him: The eyes of your understanding being enlightened; that ye may know what is the hope of his calling, and what the riches of the glory of his inheritance in the saints,*

The eyes of your understanding are the eyes of your mind – your imagination. It is a place of deep thought, meditation, indwelling, soaking, contemplation, exploration, and examination. It is the place where God instills his wisdom and revelation to be infused with knowledge of him. The imagination is also a place where you learn the strength and wealth of who you are, your inheritance, and how to walk in destiny with the Lord. Even people who have no revelation of soaking or reject soaking, are engaging in it if they have any kind of in depth revelation of God and who they are in him. The eyes of their understanding have been enlightened through deep contemplation and exploration of him and his presence.

Hebrews **5:14** lets us know that we should exercise our senses to strengthen our discernment of knowing what is good and what is evil. Your senses (see, hear, taste, smell, feel) entail your ability to perceive, understand and judge. The word *"exercise"* is *Gymanazo* in the Greek and means *"to practice naked, train."* Naked insinuates a place of vulnerability. Essentially God is encouraging you to expose yourself through the art of soaking with him so you can be enlightened, cultivated, and solidified in what is of him and what is not of him. You need your imagination to soak. As your spirit becomes one with God, he will begin to reveal what he is doing in your spirit through your imagination. The more you exercise the enlightenment of your imagination with God, the less vain and evil imaginations you will encounter, and the easier it will be to cast down vain and evil imaginations when they come. It will also be easier to set your affections on things above and to live from a heavenly perspective with Christ Jesus.

> *Ephesians* **2:6** *And hath raised us up together, and made us sit together in heavenly places in Christ Jesus*

> *Ephesians* **1:3** *Blessed be the God and Father of our Lord Jesus Christ, who has blessed us in Christ with every spiritual blessing in the heavenly realms.*

Exercising Your Imagination Activation:

1. What religious myths or errors have you been taught regarding your imagination?
2. Cast down these myths and errors by spending time in prayer falling out of agreement with them.
3. Spend time using the blood of Jesus to cleanse out all pride, evil, sin, worldliness, compromise and desensitization out of your imagination and senses (example: With the blood of Jesus I cleanse all lust and pornography from TV out of my imagination, eye gates, ear gates, sense of smell, sense of touch, feelings, and emotions).
4. Using the scripture regarding being seated in heavenly places, spend time resting before God and asking him to fill your imagination with what that scripture entails and how to live from that place.
5. Using the fruit of the spirit in Galatians, spend time setting your affections on them and asking God to fill your imagination with his character, nature, and expressions of them for people, the land, and world at large. *Galatians 5:22-23 But the fruit of the Spirit is love, joy, peace, longsuffering, gentleness, goodness, faith, Meekness, temperance: against such there is no law.*

MOVE ME JESUS!

Move me beyond worldliness
Move me beyond lust
Move me beyond flesh
Move in me Lord

Move me beyond carnality
Move me beyond the superficial
Move me beyond fellowship
I want only Godly relations
Move in me Lord

Move me beyond gossip
Purge my tongue with Your anointing oil
Move me beyond the realistic
Supernaturally, move in me Lord

Move me beyond sin
Mold me in Your perfect love
Move me beyond the immediate
Move in me Lord

Move me beyond the comprehendible
Do a miraculous work from the inside out
Move me beyond the conventional
Make me of Your peculiar people
Move in me Lord

Move me beyond what I am
Move me beyond who I will be
Move me into divine destiny
My Dear Lord, Move in me

Move Me! Love You Jesus!
By: Taquetta Baker

HOW TO SOAK & FEAST!

You can soak while:
- ➤ *Taking walks*
- ➤ *Lying down*
- ➤ *Resting in a chair or quiet place*
- ➤ *Taking soak breaks by inviting God to commune with you throughout the day*
- ➤ *Transitioning to sleep at night*

Often, we have been told we must be lying down to soak and feast in the presence of the Lord, and though this is ideal, God is not limited in how we spend intimate time with him. In Genesis, we read that God walked with Adam in the cool of the day, so God can commune and soak us in his glory even while we are taking a walk. I love to power walk and pray. I invite the Holy Spirit to walk with me and I just spend time focusing on building my relationship with Jesus and being consumed by his presence, word, fruit, identity, character and nature. Sometimes, I soak while driving although this can be hard and dangerous, and you might have to pull over depending on how strong God's presence invades your car. Throughout my day, I will invite the Holy Spirit to invade me wherever I am and saturate me. Soaking breaks are great and refreshing. Beckoning God as you go about your day builds relationship, quickens you to consider him first in your decision making, and provides opportunity to be strengthened in his might and presence.

There are other times where I do sit or lay down and soak. I love to visit with God by the fireplace or on the living room couch, and God will sometimes ask me to meet him in those places to visit with him. Often these are the times where I will ascend to the heavens and God will give me visions and strategies for my church, for people, or challenges for their lives, or he will give me visions of my future or the path he is taking me. This is also a time where God will have me focus on areas where I need deliverance and healing.

Another great opportunity where we can take advantage of soaking is when you are transitioning to sleep at night. Soaking is a great way to unwind and release the day. It also positions you in the presence of the Lord, where prophetic dreams and visions and peaceful rest is most likely to occur.

> *Soaking is a spirit to spirit exchange of transformation with God*
> *Soaking is spending time with God, while resting in the knowing that he is present and attentive even when no words are spoken or tingling feelings of his presence are experienced*
> *Soaking is about surrendering from working, while not demanding God to work as the two of you just rest in communion together*

Often, we strive to have God perform by speaking or manifesting his presence, **but since soaking is a spirit to spirit exchange of transformation, it is not about speaking or feeling**. When we are hanging with our best friends or spouses, we are not always talking and we are not always feeling loved, connected, empowered or joyful. Yet there is the knowing that our love and connection is eternal, and being together brings an empowering strength all by itself. We need to understand that just being with God is enough. It is important to learn how to value the fact that God is always with us. Therefore, it is essential to take time to just be with him - doing nothing with him, not expecting anything of him or demanding anything of ourselves, and knowing that this is enough and is just as fulfilling as if we were talking, receiving revelation, or being consumed by the weighty glory of his presence.

> *Soaking is not about disposition but composition – taking on the form of the essence of God*
> *Soaking is an active resting place in God – not performing but actively engaging in taking in his essence*
> *Soaking has no religious formula – it is guided by your love for God, drive for his presence, his love for you, and desire to fill you up with him*

Though our disposition (sitting, lying down, walking) is not the most important factor when soaking, our composition is very important. When you soak something, like a towel or sponge, its composition usually changes. What that object originally was or does, is now consumed by what absorbed it. The consumption changes the object's character and response. There is an immobility that occurs when something is soaked. It becomes overtaken by what absorbed it and becomes subject to that consumption. When we soak in the presence of God, we become consumed by his presence and subject to his essence that is absorbing us. We are no longer operating in our own strength, will, engaging in religious activities or rhetoric, or trying to plan the next act.

To be frank, there is a difference between soaking experiences and praise and worship experiences. Because we are busy people, we think we are soaking when God's presence is in our midst. *Though we can consume a measure of him and can even be transformed in this place, if we say we are soaking, then we are not working or even allowing our flesh, thoughts and emotions to dictate our interactions with God. Our spirit is engaging God and everything that occurs with us, is manifesting through our spirit to spirit encounter with him. It is a posture of taking in God and engaging him through a place of rest, surrender, and refreshing, while allowing the mind, will, emotions and physical body to be empowered and guided by the wealth and wellness of his presence.*

> ➢ *If you are up and about engaging in religious activities - praying for others, releasing a word, more engaged in the song, music, or what is happening among you than with God - then you are not soaking*
> ➢ *If your focus is more on how what God is doing is making you feel than being transformed in what he is doing then you are not soaking*

Even as Adam and Eve walked in the cool of the day with God, they were not working, performing, or proving anything. They were relaxing and absorbing the sound, breath, wind, word, essence and will of God. This is the reason Adam and Eve hid in the garden. They had eaten of the tree of good and evil. Their composition had changed from being totally like God and taking in more of him, to having a fashion of Satan and the world. Until this point, they had the honor of simply reigning in the presence of the Lord. After partaking of the knowledge of good and evil, Adam and Eve were keenly aware of their flesh and emotions, and did not know how to surrender them to the presence of God. Originally, they fully possessed the character, nature, and essence of God and were being further cultivated in his likeness. They did not have to be conscious of surrendering, nor did they have to learn how to. Partaking of the tree changed their composition and the composition of mankind. Though Jesus restored our salvation and right to commune in eternity with God, we must engage in relationship with him, such that our nature and character is consumed by his presence and likeness, and we learn to be surrendered inside our rightful place of intimacy with him. Soaking is therefore about resting inside the presence of God and becoming what is of him.

Soaking & Feasting Exploration:
1. Journal five characteristics of true soaking.

2. What is the difference between a soaking experience and a worship experience?
3. What are some of your biggest challenges to experiencing the true art of soaking?
4. What do you need to surrender to really yield to cultivating a soaking lifestyle?
5. Spend time relinquishing those areas of yourself and life to God.

THE HOLY PURSUIT

Another facet of soaking entails a pursuit of the presence and benefactors of God's glory. This pursuit is with your soul and/or your spirit. Your soul and spirit is communing and seeking God's wealth that is inside his presence. This is not a striving or an act of working. It is from a posture of communing with God, asking him to soak you in an area, and meditating on God or that area of God, as he fulfills your desire by consuming and transforming you in that area.

> *Psalms 27:4-6 One thing have I desired of the Lord, that will I seek after; that I may dwell in the house of the Lord all the days of my life, to behold the beauty of the Lord, and to enquire in his temple. For in the time of trouble he shall hide me in his pavilion: in the secret of his tabernacle shall he hide me; he shall set me up upon a rock. And now shall mine head be lifted up above mine enemies round about me: therefore will I offer in his tabernacle sacrifices of joy; I will sing, yea, I will sing praises unto the Lord.*

> *Psalms 42:1-4 To the chief Musician, Maschil, for the sons of Korah. As the hart panteth after the water brooks, so panteth my soul after thee, O God. My soul thirsteth for God, for the living God: when shall I come and appear before God? My tears have been my meat day and night, while they continually say unto me, Where is thy God? When I remember these things, I pour out my soul in me: for I had gone with the multitude, I went with them to the house of God, with the voice of joy and praise, with a multitude that kept holyday.*

Sometimes we long to be in the presence of God – thirsting for a drink of him -desiring to have more of him – look more like him – be more like him – act like him. This is perfectly alright as God desires to reveal himself to and through his people.

> **Jeremiah 33:3** *Call to Me and I will answer you, and I will tell you great and mighty things, which you do not know.*

> **Proverbs 25:2** *It is the glory of God to conceal a matter, But the glory of kings is to search out a matter.*

> **Amos 3:7** *Surely the Lord GOD does nothing Unless He reveals His secret counsel To His servants the prophets.*

> **1Corinthians 2:10** *For to us God revealed them through the Spirit; for the Spirit searches all things, even the depths of God.*

> **Ephesians 1:9** *He made known to us the mystery of His will, according to His kind intention which He purposed in Him.*

There are mysteries, revelations, answers, strategies, blessings, deliverance, healing, fruits, powers, wonders, abilities, and benefits hidden inside the presence of God that we need and that God wants to give us.

> **Psalms 103:1-5** *Bless the Lord, O my soul: and all that is within me, bless his holy name. Bless the Lord, O my soul, and forget not all his benefits: Who forgiveth all thine iniquities; who healeth all thy diseases; Who redeemeth thy life from destruction; who crowneth thee with lovingkindness and tender mercies; Who satisfieth thy mouth with good things; so that thy youth is renewed like the eagle's.*

David did not want to be separated from the benefits that came with living in God and pursuing his presence. Everything about him blessed God and wanted God's purpose and will for his life. David also understood that everything he needed was inside of God and that he was nothing without him. We must have this pursuit as well and seek God for ways to be filled up and transformed in him.

When you are in pursuit to be filled up in God or filled with a benefactor of God, you can ask him for what you desire then spend time soaking yourself in that area. Sometimes I just spend a few minutes throughout the day soaking myself in various areas that I desire to be cultivated, empowered, or transformed in.

❖ *Soak in the Blood of Jesus* to receive cleansing. The blood of Jesus purges, purifies, redeems, reconciles, sanctifies, sanitizes, forgives, heals, and frees you from death (***Ephesians 1:7** Whom we have redemption through his blood, the forgiveness of sins, according to the riches of his grace*). We hear a lot about pleading the blood, but the blood is an application. Jesus applied his blood to our sins and sicknesses, and through his perfected blood, we were redeemed and made whole. You can apply the blood of Jesus to your soul, heart, mind, thoughts, personality, character, identity, righteousness and body, and command redemption, life, and wholeness to come. You can soak yourself in the blood until you see breakthrough in these areas, or as a daily application of being cleansed and free in God.

❖ *Soak to be Baptized in the Holy Spirit and Fire of God.* This dimension of fire burns up everything that is not like God, while infusing you with his Holy Spirit and fire that eternally dwells inside of you where Jesus and his kingdom is continually evident and exposed to the world. (***Matthew 3:11-12** I indeed baptize you with water unto repentance. but he that cometh after me is mightier than I, whose shoes I am not worthy to bear: he shall baptize you with the Holy Ghost, and with fire: Whose fan is in his hand, and he will*

*throughly purge his floor, and gather his wheat into the garner;
but he will burn up the chaff with unquenchable fire).*
Sometimes it takes consistent communing and pursuit of
the baptism of the Holy Spirit and Fire to receive it. Be
persistent and earnest in your motives and desires and
God will give you the desires of your heart in this area.

❖ **Soak to be Infused with the Deliverance and Healing fire
of God.** The fire of God burns out, fuses, refines, purges,
purifies, consumes, and tests (**Malachi 3:2-3** *But who may
abide the day of his coming? and who shall stand when he
appeareth? for he is like a refiner's fire, and like fullers' soap:
And he shall sit as a refiner and purifier of silver: and he shall
purify the sons of Levi, and purge them as gold and silver, that
they may offer unto the Lord an offering in righteousness).*
Sometimes you will cast out demons, but their deposits
and attributes are still lodged in you. Use the fire of God
to purge and burn out these demonic deposits. You can
also purify and refine yourself with the fire of God.
Demons hate the fire of God and the blood of Jesus. Fire is
judgment to demons. You can use the fire of God to
torment demons and send them fleeing from your life,
blood line, ministry, land, atmosphere, and region.
(**Revelations 20:10** *And the devil that deceived them was cast
into the lake of fire and brimstone, where the beast and the false
prophet are, and shall be tormented day and night for ever and
ever).*

❖ **Soak to Receive the Mysteries of the Kingdom (Ephesians
1:9).** Receive:
  o Revelations
  o Knowledge
  o Wisdom
  o Insight/Direction
  o Strategies
  o Tools
  o Answers

- o Prophecies
- o Visions
- o Divine Visitations
- o Translated in the spirit
- o Experiences to heaven
- o Insight into the demonic realm
- o Angelic Encounters

Make sure the Holy Spirit is leading you and you are not engaging in these experiences illegally.

- ❖ *Soak your Soul, Heart, Mind or Body to Receive Deliverance, Healing and Transformation.* Sometimes God desires to commune with us so rather than allowing speedy healing, soaking will be needed to process you to breakthrough. Be content if this is God's method of breakthrough for you. You will not be disappointed as you commune with him, learn of him, learn about yourself, and partake of his presence (*Psalms 23:3, Psalms 147:3, Jeremiah 30:17, Matthew 11:28, Romans 12:2*).

- ❖ *Soak in the Fruit of the Spirit* to build your character, nature, and identity in God. The fruit of the spirit also fills, restores, produces, and reproduces. With the blood of Jesus, cleanse yourself of all defiled, demonic, and unhealthy fruit that does not represent the character and nature of God, while filling yourself up in all the fruit that represents his character, nature and identity (*Galatians 5:22-23*).

- ❖ *Soaking Divine Growth and Maturity.* Soaking in the presence of the Lord can cause an acceleration anointing to come upon you, such that you mature and are equipped faster in his purpose and will for your life. It can also SHIFT you to dimensions of his glory that you would not attain at ministry events or general experiences in his presence. (*1Corinthians 3:18And all of us, as with unveiled face, [because we] continued to behold [in the Word of God] as in a mirror the glory of the Lord, are constantly being transfigured into His very own image in ever increasing splendor and from one degree of glory to another; [for this comes] from the Lord [Who is] the Spirit).*

❖ *Soaking your Mantle, Calling and Giftings* in the will, purpose, plan, or prophecies that have been spoken over your life. Sometimes these areas need to be cleansed, or renewed, refreshed, empowered, and awakened through the art of soaking and communing with God. There are instances where I soak these areas to cleanse from warfare of past seasons. Especially if I have incurred soul and heart wounds, or physical ailments due to wear and tear to my body or from persecution of the gospel. I will also spend time soaking in prophecies that have been spoken over my life or to strengthen or cultivate my mantle, calling, or gifting in an area (*1Corinthians 12, 1Corinthians 14:1, 1Peter1:10, Ephesians 4, Isaiah 60:1, Jeremiah 29:11*).

❖ *Soak in the Power of God* as it is your kingly right to be infused with limitless power. The power of God delivers, overthrows demonic powers and governments, releases the virtue and government of God, releases miracles, signs, and wonders (*Acts 1:8 But ye shall receive power, after that the Holy Ghost is come upon you: and ye shall be witnesses unto me both in Jerusalem, and in all Judaea, and in Samaria, and unto the uttermost part of the earth*). Use the power of God to annihilate the powers of the enemy (*Luke 10:19 Behold, I give unto you power to tread on serpents and scorpions, and over all the power of the enemy: and nothing shall by any means hurt you*). Study the power of God as you will find that you can recreate and create body parts, birth forth things that you need, bring excellency to your heart, mind and soul, release virtue into your life, and annihilate the power of the enemy such that it brings deliverance and healing.

❖ *Soak in the Glory of God* so you can always be filled up in him. Whatever we need and desire from God is inside his glory. The Glory refreshes, fills, refills, fulfills, creates, recreates, revives, renews, makes whole, establishes the presence of God, and draws us into intimacy and relationship with God, while instilling God's character, nature, truth, knowledge, revelation, and pleasures forevermore (**Psalms 16:11** *Thou wilt shew me the path of life: in thy presence is fulness of joy; at thy right hand there are pleasures for evermore*). You should be living inside the presence of God. This is where your direction of life is revealed. As you walk in alignment with God, continual fulness of joy and pleasures of God should be evident in your life. If you live in the glory of God, you should be living a fulfilled life no matter what trials and tribulations may occur. Ask God for revelation on how to build a relationship with him where you abide in his presence. Use his presence to refresh, fulfill, and fill you. Continually cultivate your life and atmosphere in his presence so you can be a true glory carrier (**John 15:4** *Abide in me, and I in you. As the branch cannot bear fruit of itself, except it abide in the vine; no more can ye, except ye abide in me*).

❖ *Rivers of Living Water* as God's rivers stirs, replenishes, breeds life, vitality, beauty, youthfulness, creativity, strength, efficiency, and releases what is inside of you to whatever you are sending it to (**John. 7:38** *He that believeth on me, as the scripture hath said, out of his belly shall flow rivers of living water*). It is important to spend time cleansing and stir the rivers that are inside of you, such that the wells that you flow out of are pure, as whatever is in you will be released to those you minister too.

❖ *Soaking Intercessory Prayer* Soaking prayer can also be a great tool when praying for someone who needs deep or inner healing. Usually I sit the person down or have them lie down and ask the Holy Spirit to come consume them. If there are specific areas where they need healing, I ask the Holy Spirit to come and bring healing to those areas. I may also apply the blood of Jesus or the fire of the Holy Ghost to cleanse or heal those areas. Soaking intercessory prayers take longer, but they are a great way to demonstrate God's love, power, and birth forth miracles in areas where there may be hidden roots, embedded strongholds, or the person needs to experience the unconditional love of God.

The Lord may lead you in what to speak or may require no words at all. He may unction you to release love, peace, life, or rest to a person. Or the Lord may lead you to sing or dance around the person as a way of soaking and saturating them in his presence. As you pray, you can use visualizations to help the person in receiving revelation of what God is doing or simply encourage the person to rest and trust God to work in them. Let the person remain in soaking prayer until the Spirit tells you it is time to bring them back into the present time and place and be open to allowing the person to spend alone time resting and feasting in the fullness of the Lord. Remember God hungers to be intimate with us. It is his desire just as much as it is ours.

RELINQUISHING CONTROL

- If you are not succumbing to him, then you are working or striving rather than soaking
- If you are more focused on what is occurring around you, then you are not soaking
- If you are more consumed by doing or what you should be doing then you are not soaking
- If you are focused on life issues and tasks and how to complete, fix, or solve them, then you are not soaking

Engaging in any of these areas, takes you out of the absorbing place of God and SHIFTS you into the composition of whatever is consuming you. It also increases your anxiety and zaps you of strength rather than SHIFTING you to a place of refreshing and enduring faith in him.

Matthew 11:28-30 Come to me, all who labor and are heavy laden, and I will give you rest. Take my yoke upon you, and learn from me, for I am gentle and lowly in heart, and you will find rest for your souls. For my yoke is easy, and my burden is light.

(The Amplified Version) Come to Me, all you who labor and are heavy-laden and overburdened, and I will cause you to rest. [I will ease and relieve and refresh your souls.] Take My yoke upon you and learn of Me, for I am gentle (meek) and humble (lowly) in heart, and you will find rest (relief and ease and refreshment and recreation and blessed quiet) for your souls. For My yoke is wholesome (useful, good--not harsh, hard, sharp, or pressing, but comfortable, gracious, and pleasant), and My burden is light and easy to be borne.

(The Message Version) Are you tired? Worn out? Burned out on religion? Come to me. Get away with me and you'll recover your life. I'll show you how to take a real rest. Walk with me and work with me — watch how I do it. Learn the unforced rhythms of grace. I won't lay anything heavy or ill-fitting on you. Keep company with me and you'll learn to live freely and lightly."

Labor is *Kopiao* in the Greek and means:
1. to feel fatigue; by implication, to work hard
2. (bestow) labor, toil, be wearied, bestow labor
3. to grow weary, tired, exhausted (with toil or burdens or grief)
4. to labor with wearisome effort, to toil

Heavy Laden is *Phortizo* in the Greek and means:
1. to load up (properly, as a vessel or animal), i.e. (figuratively) to overburden with ceremony (or spiritual anxiety)
2. lade, by heavy laden, to place a burden upon, to load
3. metaph. to load one with a burden (of rites and unwarranted precepts)

We must cease with laboring when soaking in the presence of God. We must also seek to release every burden and load upon him, while exchanging them for the fruit and strength of his presence.

Rest in this scripture is the Hebrew word *Katapausis* and means:
1. reposing down, i.e. (by Hebraism) abode
2. a putting to rest calming of the winds, a resting place
3. metaph. the heavenly blessedness in which God dwells, and of which he has promised to make persevering believers in Christ partakers after the toils and trials of life on earth are ended

Dictionary.com defines *Repose* as:
1. to lie at rest
2. to lie dead
3. to remain still or concealed
4. to take a rest
5. to rest for support: lie

As you can see, resting is not working or striving. It is literally a posture of sleep or death, where we are totally surrendered to the presence of God, and trusting him with our very being.

The ultimate key to soaking is total abandonment to the Holy Spirit. One must give up the need to control and dictate to truly grow in this level of prayer. God wants us naked before him. He wants us vulnerable. Not so he can shame us in who we are, but because he simply desires to commune with the realness of our existence and release us from the shame that was put on us through sin, so that we can be perfected in his image.

Another word for *Rest* in the Greek is *Anapauo* and means:
1. to cause or permit one to cease from any movement or labor to recover and collect his strength
2. to give rest, refresh, to give one's self rest, take rest
3. to keep quiet, of calm and patient expectation

To truly rest, you must totally relinquish all control. When it comes to resting in God, you must completely lodge in the presence of God almost to a state of sleeping or dying. You relinquish control while allowing God to guide your time. Truly this is how our total walk with the Lord is to be, yet because we tend to feel like we must work to get God to move, we end up controlling, dictating and determining the outcome of situations, rather than letting God be the driver of our journey. The inability to relinquish control can be a serious hindrance to soaking with God and if there is a challenge or stronghold in your life in this area, it will cause agitation when attempting to rest and bask in the presence of the Lord.

> **2Samuel 6:14-15** *And David danced before the LORD with all [his] might; and David [was] girded with a linen ephod. So David and all the house of Israel brought up the ark of the LORD with shouting, and with the sound of the trumpet. So David and all the house of Israel brought up the ark of the LORD with shouting, and with the sound of the trumpet.*

> **Verse 20-23** *Then David returned to bless his household. And Michal the daughter of Saul came out to meet David, and said, How glorious was the king of Israel to day, who uncovered himself to day in the eyes of the handmaids of his servants, as one of the vain fellows shamelessly uncovereth himself! And David said unto Michal, [It was] before the LORD, which chose me before thy father, and before all his house, to appoint me ruler over the people of the LORD, over Israel: Therefore will I play before the LORD. And I will yet be more vile than thus, and will be base in mine own sight: and of the maidservants which thou hast spoken of, of them shall I be had in honour. Therefore Michal the daughter of Saul had no child unto the day of her death.*

Wikipedia Online Encyclopedia describes the *ephod* as *"a priestly linen garment that was worn by ordinary priest."* It was not really seen as clothing or a complete garment. In my terms, David had on his pajamas in public and others have even said he was basically naked. Usually only those we have a personal relationship with tend to see us in our pajamas, and though David most likely did not have a personal relationship with all the house of Israel, he had one with God and was demonstrating his freedom, love, and intimacy with him shamelessly and abandoned. *Psalms 42:1* gives us a glimpse of how David felt about God.

> *"As the hart panteth after the water brooks, so panteth my soul after thee, O God. My soul thirsteth for God, for the living God: when shall I come and appear before God?"*

Though David was not alone soaking in *2Samuel 6*, his private worship had obviously become public as he was basking in the presence of the Lord with all that was in him and for all the world to see. He was having such a good time that he was not dressed in his kingly apparel and thus exposed himself as he was dancing. His wife watched from the window and was ashamed of his actions. We can discern from her reaction that she did not have the level of relationship that David had with the Lord, and did not like that he was vulnerable and exposed in the presence of the Lord and especially the people. But David loved the Lord so and was a man after God's own heart till he did not care, and declared that he would be even more defiled and debased than he was. David knew the benefits of engulfing God and he knew how to feast of his pleasures. It will take being vulnerable before King Jesus to feast in the pleasures of his fullness.

Please be aware that because soaking prayer is deep intimacy with the presence of God, and flesh cannot glory in the presence of the Lord (*1Corinthians 1:29*), that it will reveal every defense mechanism, trust issue, insecurity and vulnerability you have. The Holy Spirit is a comforter, he will not push more on you than you are willing to receive so please know, that he is willing to build a trusting relationship with you so that you can be free among him. However, the more you hang on to baggage, the longer it keeps you from entering the fullness of intimacy and wholeness in God. The more you are willing to relinquish and flow in the process of building an open relationship with God, the deeper you will soak and see his presence in your everyday life.

Relinquishing Control Activation:

1. Do you have control issues? Explain your answer.
2. Journal the experiences where you relinquished control and they resulted in a negative outcome.
3. Journal experiences where you did not relinquish control but should have and they resulted in a negative outcome.
4. What does it feel like when you cannot control a situation?
5. What thoughts do you have about yourself and God when you cannot control a situation?
6. What thoughts and feelings do you have when having to relinquish control to a person?
7. What thoughts and feelings do you have regarding having to relinquish control to God?
8. Do you trust God? Explain your answer.
9. What does it mean when we say, "God is the head/Lord of your life?"
10. Is God the head of your life? Explain your answer.
11. What needs to be SHIFTED in you where God is the complete Lord of your life?
12. What thoughts and feelings are you experiencing as you answer these questions?
13. Spend time sharing your thoughts and feelings with God.
14. Journal your experience in prayer and what God shares with you.

Faith Building Activation

1. Relinquishing control is about having unwavering faith in God. Do a scripture study on faith.

2. Decree those scriptures out loud three times a week
3. Spend time soaking yourself in those scriptures until you have built sufficient unwavering faith of God.
4. Seek God before making any decisions in your life and practice being obedient to what he says.
5. Share what God says with a reliable source who can keep you accountable to being obedient to God and being led by him.

EXPOSING & CONQUERING HINDRANCES TO SOAKING

- **Fear** – *2 Timothy 1:7 For God hath not given us the spirit of fear; but of power, and of love, and of a sound mind.* Fear is not of God. Fear can be a spirit or an overwhelming thought or feeling that has a stronghold in your heart, mind and soul. Basically, if you are challenged with fear, then that feeling or thought has become greater than God in your life (vain imagination). Fear will have to be cast out or cast down if you want to cultivate a soaking lifestyle.

- **Fear of the Unknown**
  o God will not take you anywhere in him that you are not ready or willing to go.
  o God will not take you anywhere in him that he has not equipped or mantled you to handle.
  o There is nothing to fear about intimacy with God. He will never leave you, forsake you, or harm you (**Hebrews 13:5**).

- **Resistance to Being Vulnerable** – We fear being vulnerable because it leaves us susceptible to being hurt, wounded, attacked, criticized, tempted, etc. We tend to be offensive in our effort to avoid pain and trials, yet this causes defensive walls and blockages in our relationship with God. God is going to tell you the truth about yourself. But it is never to tear you down. It is always to strip you of everything that is preventing you from being the greatest you possible and from operating in your fullest potential. *Jeremiah 29:11-13 For I know the thoughts that I think toward you, saith the Lord, thoughts of peace, and not of evil, to give you an expected end. Then shall ye call upon me, and ye shall go and pray unto me, and I will hearken unto you. And ye shall seek me, and find me, when ye shall search for me with all your heart.* Thoughts in this passage of scripture means *"devices, purpose, plans, inventions."* You can be vulnerable with God. God has greatness in store for you and an expected end that is for your good and for his glory.

- **Challenges with Relinquishing Control** – the challenge with control is it results in us playing two roles – playing the role of God while also playing the role of self. We can never be God. The shoes are too big to fill. Moreover, filling two roles in our lives cause clashes and messes that we claim we were striving to avoid through our effort to control everything. *Proverbs 19:21 Many are the plans in a person's heart, but it is the LORD's purpose that prevails.* Our plans and intentions are good but it is only what God has purposed that will triumph and last. Soaking is one of the greatest tools to helping you relinquish total control of your life to God, where we not only have great plans, but prevail in purpose and destiny unveiled in our lives.

- **Trust & Faith Issues** – Often trust and faith issues are due to unresolved painful experiences where people have broken vows or commitments. They are also due to unresolved areas of rejection, abandonment, misuse, abuse, and/or loss of control and rights. We must understand that though God wants to heal our wounds, he is not those people. We cannot have an intimate relationship with God without faith and trust and cannot blame and reject him because of the mistakes of others. Trust and faith go hand and hand and are essential for believing in God, that he saved you, that he delivered you, that he healed you, and that he can further SHIFT you into living through the full conversion of his work as your savior. Sometimes when people have a difficult time trusting God, they are uneasy with how his presence feels. They may not be accustomed to pure love, kindness, realness in relationship interactions and commune that is void of impure motives. Some may have a difficult time trusting that it is the essence of God, and being vulnerable in his presence. There may also be a fear of the Holy Spirit, fear of what others around them will say, or how they will react if they surrender to the Holy Spirit.

- o **Psalms 9:10** *To Know Him Is to Trust Him.*
- o **Hebrews 1:1** *Now faith is the substance of things hoped for, the evidence of things not seen.*
- o **Hebrews 11:6** *But without faith it is impossible to please him: for he that cometh to God must believe that he is, and that he is a rewarder of them that diligently seek him.*
- o **James 2:17 NIV** *Now faith is the substance of things hoped for, the evidence of things not seen.*

Soaking teaches you about God and develops and cultivates your faith in him.

If trust and a lack of faith is your issue, I suggest using a simple technique I call *"I Trust You Jesus."*

➤ Simply take one minute to breathe in and out deeply to help clear your mind and surrender to the thought of resting and trusting.

➤ If you speak in tongues, then spend a few minutes speaking in your prayer language.

➤ Take deep breathes in and out while focusing on the love of God.

➤ After a minute, take a deep breathe while verbally releasing your life, experiences, and situations to God - telling him, *"I trust you Jesus."*

For Example:

- Inhale and Exhale and then say, "I Trust You God with my Kids!"
- Inhale and Exhale and then say, I Trust You God with my Home!"

- Inhale and Exhale and then say, "I Trust You God with my Job!"
- Inhale and Exhale and then say, "I Trust You God with my ministry!"
- Inhale and Exhale and then say, "I Trust You God with my Gifts."
- Inhale and Exhale and then say, "I Trust You God with my Car."
- Inhale and Exhale and then say, "I Trust You God with my Purpose."

And on and on they go while surrendering to the presence of God. After about five minutes of this, you should be able to focus on God, enjoying his presence, and engaging in communion with him. If not,

- Repent for stress and areas you do not trust God; cleanse those areas with the blood of Jesus.
- Return to completing the trust technique again, while surrendering whatever you need to release to the Lord. You can even release hurts, pains, fears, grief, loss, anxiety, pride, etc.
- Focus again on God and engage him in communion.
- Practice this daily until you learn to surrender to God's presence without fear or hesitancy.
- As you are soaking, ask God to show you areas where you need to surrender your life to him and how to trust and build faith in him.
- Ask him to show you experiences where your trust and faith was broken, and allow him to heal those areas inside his presence.

- **Restlessness** - The soul, mind, heart, body, and spirit can be restless. There also can be a demonic spirit of restlessness operating within us or a spirit of affliction that causes restlessness. Worries, stress, tiredness, fear, challenging situations, and witchcraft can cause restlessness. In this day and age, it can be difficult to avoid restlessness. One of the ways to combat restlessness is to soak yourself to sleep at night and even take soaking breaks throughout the day, while cleansing yourself of everything that causes restlessness. Praise and worship also combats restlessness. Once the heaviness has lifted through praise, you can spend time cleaning all restlessness and soaking in the refreshing power of God.

Dictionary.com defines *Restlessness* as:
1. characterized by or showing inability to remain at rest
2. unquiet or uneasy, as a person, the mind, or the heart
3. never at rest; perpetually agitated or in motion
4. without rest; without restful sleep
5. unceasingly active; averse to quiet or inaction, as persons

- ○ ***Psalms 28:6-10 (The Amplified Version)*** *I am bent and bowed down greatly; I go about mourning all the day long. For my loins are filled with burning; and there is no soundness in my flesh. I am faint and sorely bruised [deadly cold and quite worn out]; I groan by reason of the disquiet and moaning of my heart. Lord, all my desire is before You; and my sighing is not hidden from You. My heart throbs, my strength fails me; as for the light of my eyes, it also is gone from me.*
- ○ ***Psalms 42:11*** *Why art thou cast down, O my soul? and why art thou disquieted in me? hope thou in God: for I shall yet praise him for the help of his countenance.*
- ○ ***Psalms 77:3-10*** *I remembered God, and was troubled: I complained, and my spirit was overwhelmed. Selah. Thou holdest mine eyes waking: I am so troubled that I cannot speak. I have considered the days of old, the years of ancient times. I call to remembrance my song in the night: I commune with mine own heart: and my spirit made diligent search. Will the Lord cast off for ever? and will he be favorable no more? Is his mercy clean gone for ever? doth his promise fail for evermore?*

Hath God forgotten to be gracious? hath he in anger shut up his tender mercies? Selah. And I said, This is my infirmity: but I will remember the years of the right hand of the most High.

o **1Peter 5:10** *And after you have suffered a little while, the God of all grace [Who imparts all blessing and favor], Who has called you to His [own] eternal glory in Christ Jesus, will Himself complete and make you what you ought to be, establish and ground you securely, and strengthen, and settle you.*

➢ If your mind continues to race, pray boldly in your prayer language until you feel your mind coming to a place of peace.

➢ Use Christian soaking music or scriptures that can fill your atmosphere with the presence of God so you can focus on him or an area in him.

➢ Sometimes, racing thoughts could be God leading you to explore a certain subject during your soaking time. If you attempt to soak and keep focusing on a subject or situation, ask God if this is something he desires you to focus on during your prayer time. Sometimes, God will give us a strong urge or thought towards a situation where he may want to provide clarity, healing, or wisdom.

➢ Racing thoughts can also be a demonic blockage that is hindering you from entering the presence of God. If this is the case, binding the blocking spirit and casting it from between you and Jesus will clear the airways so that you can enter God's presence. Loosing the blood of Jesus to clear the airways between you and God will also remove blockages. Also, be aware that some witchcraft curses and word curses can block communication between you and the Lord. Break these witchcraft spells and word curses as necessary so you can have free access to God. You can also ask God to reveal and clear away anything that is between you and him.

➢ Sometimes, racing thoughts are due to worries,

stress, fears, anxiousness, confusion, or we carry burdens that Jesus should carry. Cast your cares by repenting for carrying them and allowing gateways to stress, fears, etc. and give them to God. While repenting, use the *Surrendering Technique* to submit your thoughts to God. The *Surrendering Technique* is quite simple.

- While taking deep breaths in and out, verbally surrendering everything to God, especially those things that are hindering you from entering a place of rest.

An example would be:
- I surrender my job (deep breath)
- I surrender my kids (deep breath)
- I surrender my finances (deep breath)
- I surrender the stress of the day (deep breath)
- I surrender my problems (deep breath)

Though my example is general, be specific regarding the situations, challenges, thoughts and emotions you are surrendering. The more you surrender your circumstances, challenges, emotions, and thoughts to God – giving them to him, the more you will be able to rest and refresh in God's spirit.

- **Anxiety/Worry/Fretting** – This can be distress, uneasiness, annoyance, irritation, agitation, or discontentment of the mind, heart, emotions, body and soul caused by perceived or real fear of danger or misfortune. The challenge with these negative attributes is that they gnaw, vex, torment, and wear on the mind, heart, emotions, body, and soul, and can cause corrosion and erosion in these areas. They become as turmoil, commotion, or pestilence within a person's imagination. The disturbance is so tormenting that it can grip the person, inciting fear, dread, confusion, discombobulation, instability and sometimes sickness. Anxiety, worry, and fretting can sometimes be caused by a demonic spirit, bewitchment or witchcraft. It also can be caused by a need to control, lack of faith and trust, and being so busy that you start to burnout. Utilize the suggestions listed for releasing control, dealing with faith and trust, and restlessness to address these areas. Surrendering yourself to God through the art of soaking also dismantles these negative attributes.

- o *Philippians 4:6-7 (The Amplified Version) Do not fret or have any anxiety about anything, but in every circumstance and in everything, by prayer and petition (definite requests), with thanksgiving, continue to make your wants known to God. And God's peace [shall be yours, that tranquil state of a soul assured of its salvation through Christ, **and so fearing** nothing from God and being content with its earthly lot of whatever sort that is, that peace] which transcends all understanding shall garrison and mount guard over your hearts and minds in Christ Jesus.*

- **Tiredness/Weariness** - Sometimes we can be too tired or weary to focus – this will need to be cleansed and burdens will need to be surrendered to rest in God's presence.

- **Burdens & Assignments Operating as Grief & Sadness –** Grief and sadness can boggle the soul and make you feel as if you are dying. Jesus asked God to take the cup he was burdened with from him. The cup entailed his assignment. It was weighing on him. God did not take the assignment from Jesus. He did send an angel to minister to him. Jesus processed through in the presence of God, while surrendering to the assignment. He drank the cup of destiny. When he surrendered to the will of God and what he was called to do, a SHIFT occurred in his spirit and he was confident in facing all that was ahead of him.

- o *Matthew 26:38-42 Then saith he unto them, My soul is exceeding sorrowful, even unto death: tarry ye here, and watch with me. And he went a little further, and fell on his face, and prayed, saying, O my Father, if it be possible, let this cup pass from me: nevertheless not as I will, but as thou wilt. And he cometh unto the disciples, and findeth them asleep, and saith unto Peter, What, could ye not watch with me one hour? Watch and pray, that ye enter not into temptation: the spirit indeed is willing, but the flesh is weak. He went away again the second time, and prayed, saying, O my Father, if this cup may not pass away from me, except I drink it, thy will be done.*
- o *Mark 14:34-36 And saith unto them, My soul is exceeding sorrowful unto death: tarry ye here, and watch. And he went forward a little, and fell on the ground, and prayed that, if it were possible, the hour might pass from him. And he said, Abba, Father, all things are possible unto thee; take away this cup from me: nevertheless not what I will, but what thou wilt.*
- o *Luke 22:41-44 And he was withdrawn from them about a stone's cast, and kneeled down, and prayed, saying, Father, if thou be willing, remove this cup from me: nevertheless not my will, but thine, be done. And there appeared an angel unto him from heaven, strengthening him. And being in an agony he prayed more earnestly: and his sweat was as it were great drops of blood falling down to the ground.*

If you read the passages of scripture you will discern that Jesus was restless, in addition to being sorrowful unto death. He had a difficult time just resting in the presence of God as he had done in times past. Rather than remaining in God's presence, he would go where the disciples were, hoping to see them praying for him in a posture to support him, while preparing themselves for the experiences that they were about to endure. However, the disciples were sleep. Jesus rebuked them for being sleep. Though Jesus eventually broke through, due to restlessness, he had to return to commune with God twice before he received the SHIFT and transformation needed to release the thoughts and feelings he had, and be surrendered unto God's will and empowered to fulfill the destiny assignment at hand. Jesus utilized the *"Surrendering Technique,"* as he shared his situation, challenges, thoughts and feelings with God. Sometimes, we must surrender our burdens and anxieties before we can soak up God's presence.

- **Unresolved Painful or Challenging Experiences –**
  Sometimes unresolved issues tend to plague our thoughts when we are trying to relax and dreams when we are sleep. Many people tend to keep busy or use medications, alcohol and drugs in effort numb the constant experiences replaying in their imagination. This can be a challenge when attempting to soak because the experiences have become high places within the person's life. Memory recall is cued and refers to the mental process of retrieval of information from the past. It is important to break the power of memory recall and to cleanse out the triggers (cues) that continuously cause the experiences to replay in your imagination. Also spend time releasing the pain, hurt, anger, resentment, unforgiveness, need to avenge etc., to God. Then spend time soaking in his healing power. The more you heal from unresolved issues, the easier it will be to cultivate a lifestyle of soaking.

  - *Psalm 18:2 The LORD is my rock and my fortress and my deliverer, my God, my rock, in whom I take refuge, my shield, and the horn of my salvation, my stronghold.*
  - *Psalm 34:18 The LORD is near to the brokenhearted and saves the crushed in spirit*

- o *Hebrews 2:18 For because he himself has suffered when tempted, he is able to help those who are being tempted.*
- o *Romans 8:18 For I consider that the sufferings of this present time are not worth comparing with the glory that is to be revealed to us.*

- **Striving** – Those who operate in striving tend to have a need to perform, need to be perfect, or are busybodies that are task oriented and success focused. Many people who operate in striving are operating in their own strength rather than God's strength. They are also operating in their emotions, competition, and from a place of anxiety and needing to prove or need to be validated rather than through the true identity and gifting of who they are. People who strive tend to vigorously exert themselves, while trying hard to achieve goals and ambitions. They tend to be in opposition and conflict with themselves. This sounds weird but this is really what is occurring. They have placed undo pressure on themselves and even though they can achieve that which they are pursuing, they tend to go after it from a posture of fear that they will fail or that they have to prove they are worthy, rather than resting in this truth and pursing their desired goal. People who struggle with striving have a difficult time soaking in God's presence because they tend to be focused more on what they believe they must prove or complete to receive from God than just being and trusting he will fill them with what they need, or that they can ask for their desires and he will fulfill them. If this is your challenge, it would be beneficial to spend time asking God to reveal your true identity to you and to heal wounds in your identity and personality. This is essential because often striving is rooted in a broken identity and or a wounded personality. It often stems from childhood trauma in these areas or from experiences where a person's self-worth was not developed, cultivated, or validated. Until these areas are healed, soaking will be difficult and feel like work. It will be important to learn and rest in your identity so you can rely and trust in God, and learn to pursue life and destiny through him.

- o *Zechariah 4:6 Then he answered and spake unto me, saying, This is the word of the LORD unto Zerubbabel, saying, Not by might, nor by power, but by my spirit, saith the LORD of hosts.*
- o *Isaiah 40:31 But they that wait upon the LORD shall renew their strength; they shall mount up with wings as eagles; they shall run, and not be weary; and they shall walk, and not faint.*
- o *Colossians 1:29 For this purpose also I labor, striving according to His power, which mightily works within me.*
- o *Psalms 46:10 (New American Standard Version) Cease striving and know that I am God; I will be exalted among the nations, I will be exalted in the earth.*

- **Condemnation, Shame & Guilt** – When a person is bound in condemnation, shame and guilt, they have a difficult time feeling worthy of being in the presence of God or of his ability to deliver, heal and set them free. The person has placed a judgment of damnation upon themselves that God is not in agreement with nor is it the will of God; or another person or the devil has made the person feel this is of God. Even when we sin and are God's child, condemnation, shame and guilt should convict us, but to feel judged unto damnation is demonic and is the enemy's way of preventing the person from receiving the full conversion of salvation. A person has to be turned over to their sin for God to unleash damnation upon them.

  - o *Psalms 81:11-12 But my people would not hearken to my voice; and Israel would none of me. So I gave them up unto their own hearts' lust: and they walked in their own counsels.*

- *Romans 1:21-24 Because that, when they knew God, they glorified him not as God, neither were thankful; but became vain in their imaginations, and their foolish heart was darkened. Professing themselves to be wise, they became fools, And changed the glory of the uncorruptible God into an image made like to corruptible man, and to birds, and fourfooted beasts, and creeping things. Wherefore God also gave them up to uncleanness through the lusts of their own hearts, to dishonour their own bodies between themselves. (Study the entire chapter of Romans 1)*

If you have not been turned over to your sin or own way, then condemnation, shame and guilt should not bind you and hinder you in your worth with God. Draw nigh to God and ask him to cleanse these negative attributes so you can embrace the consumption of God's presence, while learning through soaking to journey in the full conversion of salvation and intimate relationship with him.

- *Romans 8:1-2 There is therefore now no condemnation to them which are in Christ Jesus, who walk not after the flesh, but after the Spirit. For the law of the Spirit of life in Christ Jesus hath made me free from the law of sin and death.*
- **Romans 8:31-39 (The Message Version)** *So, what do you think? With God on our side like this, how can we lose? If God didn't hesitate to put everything on the line for us, embracing our condition and exposing himself to the worst by sending his own Son, is there anything else he wouldn't gladly and freely do for us? And who would dare tangle with God by messing with one of God's chosen? Who would dare even to point a finger? The One who died for us — who was raised to life for us! — is in the presence of God at this very moment sticking up for us. Do you think anyone is going to be able to drive a wedge between us and Christ's love for us? There is no way! Not*

trouble, not hard times, not hatred, not hunger, not homelessness, not bullying threats, not backstabbing, not even the worst sins listed in Scripture: They kill us in cold blood because they hate you. We're sitting ducks; they pick us off one by one. None of this fazes us because Jesus loves us. I'm absolutely convinced that nothing — nothing living or dead, angelic or demonic, today or tomorrow, high or low, thinkable or unthinkable — absolutely nothing can get between us and God's love because of the way that Jesus our Master has embraced us.

- **Sin Issues** – Sin grieves the heart of God and grieves the Holy Spirit. A lot of times, this grief convicts us where we feel shame and guilt for our sins and rightfully so, as to lose the conviction of the Holy Spirit can be very dangerous. Many mistake a lack of conviction as God's grace at work or God's approval. However, a lack of conviction could very well mean you are being turned over to a reprobate mind – that God has given you over to your own will and desires. When we experience the grief of the Holy Spirit, we may fear being in the presence of God or may not feel worthy to be in the presence of God. We may also experience conviction when God's presence graces us despite our sin. Convicting repentance and a changing of behavior restores the presence and countenance of God upon our lives where we can enjoy his presence without heaviness and sorrow of heart.

  o *Ephesians 4:30-32 And do not grieve the Holy Spirit of God [but seek to please Him], by whom you were sealed and marked [branded as God's own] for the day of redemption [the final deliverance from the consequences of sin]. Let all bitterness and wrath and anger and clamor [perpetual animosity, resentment, strife, fault-finding] and slander be put away from you, along with every kind of malice [all spitefulness, verbal abuse, malevolence]. Be kind and helpful to one another, tender-hearted [compassionate, understanding], forgiving one another [readily and freely], just as God in Christ also forgave you.*

- **Demonic Blockages, Oppressions, and Possessions -** Demon infestations can make it difficult to soak in the presence of God. Demons are roamers which means they are restless and busy being messy. They also cannot handle the presence of God. They fear God, his judgment, and God's presence tends to expose and torment them. Demons will seek to keep a person from entering God's presence or distracted so they are not exposed and cast out of God's presence. Consistent deliverance of demonic infestations is essential to being free of demonic strongholds. I encourage you to learn about your right to be delivered, how it is the children's bread (*Matthew 15:22-28*), and make self-deliverance a part of your prayer lifestyle. Also seek deliverance ministry from equipped believers when needing assistance with being free of demonic strongholds.

- **Witchcraft –** Witchcraft can cause mind blinding, mind binding, mind blockages, restlessness, anxiety, heaviness, depression, sickness, racing thoughts, lustful thoughts, sexual thoughts and desires, fear, confusion, distortion of truth, mistrust, doubt, doublemindness, discombobulation, laziness, disobedience, wavering, dullness, apathy towards life or the things of God, or difficulty breaking through to success and freedom concerning the things of God. Witchcraft can come as a:
  - ➢ Curse, spell, vex, or hex
  - ➢ Word curses to stifle, oppress, influence, or bind you
  - ➢ Pressing impression that ways upon you or around you

- ➤ Piercing feeling, pain, or thought
- ➤ Mind binding or blinding where it feels like something is sitting on your head, wrapped around your head and/or body, or piercing some area of your head
- ➤ Unforeseen trap, snare, or noose around your neck, life, family, or situation (*Luke 21:34*)
- ➤ Manifestation within the atmosphere
- ➤ An unseen wall, fortress, or blockage that seems to block your natural and/or spiritual life
- ➤ Unseen wall or blockage that seems to blind or bind you where you cannot think, see or press through to God or effectively explore matters from a spiritual perspective or receive downloads from God

- ○ *Galatians 3:1 O foolish Galatians, who hath bewitched you, that ye should not obey the truth, before whose eyes Jesus Christ hath been evidently set forth, crucified among you?*
- ○ *(The Message Version) You crazy Galatians! Did someone put a hex on you? Have you taken leave of the your senses? Something crazy has happened, for it's obvious that you no longer have the crucified Jesus in clear focus in your lives. His sacrifice on the Cross was certainly set before you clearly enough.*

Often, because of the witchcraft itself and because we do not know the signs, we can experience witchcraft and not even know it. We will equate the experience to something else. Sometimes we experience the manifestations above when entering a community, region, or store that is bound by witchcraft and we do not realize that it is witchcraft. Witchcraft is being released through everything these days. It is in the clothing, on the clothing, in the food, in music, on TV, in movies, on social media, in the land, in the atmosphere – EVERYWHERE! It is becoming a normal part of society, but should not be a normal part of our lives.

Soaking prayer can break the powers of witchcraft. Soaking prayer encompasses you in the presence and power of God, while providing restoration and clarity concerning who you are and who God is to you. Initially, you may have to use the *"Trust or Surrendering Technique,* to settle you inside the presence of God. But once there, witchcraft will not have a chance.
- o *John 1:5 And the light shines in darkness; and the darkness overcame it not.*

Ask God to teach you to discern witchcraft as you go about your day. The more you know how witchcraft operates and attacks, the less you will succumb to it. You will also be able to discern clearly what is your issue or challenge and what is coming upon you unaware.

- **Lack of the Full Conversion of Salvation** - Many believe in God, but the lack full conversion of salvation, where they have SHIFTED into true covenant relationship with him. Salvation encompasses all aspects of reconciliation and restoration. Reconciliation means I exercise my right to be restored unto salvation with God. Restoration means I exercise my right to be restored in relationship with God. Many have been reconciled but:
  - ❖ Still live in blatant sin
  - ❖ Are still the head of their lives or the devil is the head of their lives
  - ❖ Do not believe or live from the truth that the cross completely saves, delivers, heals, rescues, protects, and sets them free
  - ❖ Have minimal to no remorse for sin issues
  - ❖ Repent with their mouths, but not with their heart and actions (turning from sin)

- ❖ Lack faith or only exercise faith when they want something from God
- ❖ Have not SHIFTED into cooperation with the full purpose of God
- ❖ Has not SHIFTED into a fully redeemed intimate relationship and journey with God

Each of these are an essential part of salvation and are necessary to be fully converted into a child of God. It can be difficult to feast in God's presence when you only live through a measure of salvation. Some believe they have a relationship with God but do not realize that if this was true, transformation or at least a desire to be transformed would be evident. It is difficult to have relationship with God and remain in blatant sin or to live in a measure of his salvation. Relationship with God automatically creates a hunger for fullness in him and for his presence. It will prick you to seek more of God and to long for fullness in him. I encourage you to study *2Corinthians 5:11-22* and *Ephesians 2:14-22*.

- ❖ Meditate on the scripture passages and ask God to reveal to you the truth concerning the full conversion of salvation and where you need to come into alignment regarding him being complete Lord and savior of your life.
- ❖ Ask the Holy Spirit to put his conviction in you and to convict you when sin seeks to tempt your life.
- ❖ Repent quickly and seek God for characteristics and behaviors that are pleasing to him.

DELIVERANCE FROM THE DRAMA SPIRIT

Soaking is a great way to be delivered from and avoid:

- The spirit of drama
- Generational stronghold of drama
- Drama filled experiences
- The need to being constantly intertwined with drama (soulties with drama and dramatic people)
- Creating drama so you can fix people and situations (such a person has a need to be validated, is a fixer, or is mentally unstable)

Once you know the true peace and presence of God, experience it consistently, and engage God where you can receive answers, strategies, and healthy ways to handle and resolve conflict, you will not want drama in your life.

Drama is defined as any situation or series of events having vivid, emotional, conflicting, or striking interest or results. Drama essentially is self-inflicted, emotionally inflicted, world inflicted, circumstance inflicted, fantasy inflicted, or demonic inflicted tribulation.

John 16:33 These things I have spoken unto you, that in me ye might have peace. In the world ye shall have tribulation: but be of good cheer; I have overcome the world.

(The Amplified Bible) I have told you these things, so that in Me you may have [perfect] peace. In the world you have tribulation and distress and suffering, but be courageous [be confident, be undaunted, be filled with joy]; I have overcome the world." [My conquest is accomplished, My victory abiding.]

Most drama is unnecessary and can be avoided. However:

- Some people crave drama, conflict and chaos

- Some people were born and raised in drama so they are stuck in the cycle of drama
- Some people are not content unless they are in drama (This is false delusional contentment)
- Some people have a destiny killing spirit called drama that follows them everywhere to create drama and steal their fulfillment
- Some people operate in a spirit of sabotage of drama
- Some people create drama for attention, love, belonging or to be the star in their own lifetime drama filled movie
- Some people acquire an emotional intoxication and enjoyment or sexual arousal from drama - it is their drug/pleasure of choice
- Some people are miserable so they want everyone else to be miserable too - they are drama

Drama people go from situation to situation playing roles and getting you to play roles in their movie of life. Often the movie never ends as before one situation is resolved, the person has created another scenario or SHIFTED into another role, while also creating a role for you to play.

Drama people are drainers and thieves. They suck and steal the strength, peace, hope, production, fruit, progress, and success from people, groups, families, environments, organizations and situations.

Most drama filled people have a soultie with drama, chaos, strife and turmoil. It is webbed within their soul and emotions. This makes it very difficult to be free. They have to want to be delivered and have to fall out of agreement with their soultie. Otherwise you are wasting your time with trying to help them solve their drama because by the time you help them resolve it, they have created another role for you to play in their sick unhealthy webbing.

Many drama filled people get physically sick from their own drama, but some of them become sick, restless, and anxious when there is no drama. Their physical body goes through drama withdrawal like an addict and if they do not get their fix they can be tense, shaky, edgy, and on the hunt for a drama hit. They will be emotionally imbalanced until they receive it and emotional enthralled when they receive it.

Some people have subtle drama that is less overt but still have the same challenging effects. If you are not careful and discerning, you can spend years intertwined with a person who has subtle drama. You will SHIFT from situation to situation with them, while trying to fulfill roles, duties, and offer supports that enable the person rather than provoke them to self-exploration and transformation.

Drama operates as a destiny killing spirit. Many drama filled people have destroyed lives, relationships, families, businesses, etc. They have a load of baggage attached to them where they have thwarted the success, joy, love and contentment regarding themselves and others.

- Some do not have remorse for their actions
- Some are remorseful but too bound to change it
- Some do not see their actions as wrong so they tend to display offense and awe when confronted rather than remorse
- Some blame everyone else for the actions of their drama or drama following them
- Some accept responsibility for the drama, but not what is needed to change their actions

This is a list of people impacted the most by drama filled people:

- **Fixers** - those who have a need to fix people and things.
- **Rescuers** - those who have a need to save and help everyone.
- **The Projector** - those that tend to view people, relationships, and situations as projects. They recognize a need or potential and have an unhealthy drive to fulfill it or awaken the reality of potential in a person or thing.
- **Kingdom Heirs** - those within the family lineage who are successful and persevere despite childhood adversity (e.g. poverty, unhealthy parenting, abuse, bullying, rejection, etc.). God has chosen to break and destroy generational curses and bondages but sometimes they are made to feel obligated to take care of the family.
- **Need For Love & Belonging** - those broken in their identity and self-worth who want to be loved and to belong at any cost.

These people have open doors that cause them to become victims of drama filled people. They gravitate to drama because of their own role imbalances, emotional instability, and natural ability to care, empower, and fix a person or situation. If drama is always around you, check to see if you fall into one of these categories.

> *Galatians 5:15-16 The Amplified Bible But if you bite and devour one another [in partisan strife], be careful that you [and your whole fellowship] are not consumed by one another. But I say, walk and live [habitually] in the [Holy] Spirit [responsive to and controlled and guided by the Spirit]; then you will certainly not gratify the cravings and desires of the flesh (of human nature without God).*

(The Message Version) If you bite and ravage each other, watch out – in no time at all you will be annihilating each other, and where will your precious freedom be then? My counsel is this: Live freely, animated and motivated by God's Spirit. Then you will not feed the compulsions of selfishness.

Drama seeks to consume and destroys whatever it impacts. Though it appears to care for others, it is self-gratifying and self-absorbed. It will have you thinking you are important, however, its focus is to feed its compulsions for drama.

Drama is a restless, busy, anti-submissive, idolatrous spirit. It is always focused on the next role to create and star in. Soaking prayer provides a healthy and safe way to break the strongholds of drama because it requires:

- Submission to God
- Time of rest and being still
- Self and God reflection
- A focus and surrendering to truth
- A relinquishing of control and messiness
- Submitting to how God requires one to think, feel, behave, approach, and rectify situations

Soaking also provides insight on situations and people in your life and strategies for avoiding drama and resolving drama quickly when it occurs. If you are tired of the unnecessary tribulation in your life, then soaking prayer is your key to breakthrough. I DECREE a SHIFT in your life today in being delivered from the spirit of drama and breaking free from all roles, situations, and patterns of drama. **SHIFT!**

Deliverance From Drama Activation:
1. For what reasons do you desire to be free from the spirit of drama?

2. In what ways has the spirit of drama operated in your life? What are you learning about yourself and others as you examine the pattern of drama in your life.

3. What generational strongholds of drama are in your family line?

4. What does drama fulfill for you personally?

5. If you are not the star of the drama but a supporting role, what does this fulfill for you? What areas do you need healing in to break the supporting role of drama in your life?

6. Spend time repenting for drama and/or supporting roles.

7. Renounce the spirit of drama. Renounce roles and supporting roles. Cast the spirit of drama out of your life and break all soulties with it and how it fulfills you. Dedicate those areas to God.

8. Spend time releasing areas where you need voids fulfilled to God and allowing him to fill you in those areas. Spend time soaking and surrendering your hurts, challenges, and issues to God. This may require a processing (e.g. days, weeks, months) towards complete healing, but will be so worth it.

9. Spend time soaking and surrendering yourself to God. Ask him to give you a love for obedience and surrendering your life to him. As God to break your will in this area, practice a lifestyle of obedience and only doing things at the leading and direction of him (*Psalms 51:7*). You will have to consistently soak and surrender until your character, nature, emotions and thoughts consistently display the likeness and truth of God. Be okay with the process to breakthrough. The peace that you will experience through not having drama in your life will feel weird and uncomfortable and will take some getting used to. Also, not having drama in your life will be grieving and feel like loss. It will hurt sometimes as like an addict, you will crave

drama, but the more you soak in God's presence, the more you will crave him and his will rather than drama.

10. Ask God to give you a love for his peace and the ability to discern his peace from false peace. Live a lifestyle of guarding your peace and not allowing the world, people, and circumstances to steal the peace that Jesus has given you.

SOAKING MEDITATION

When meditating, we are engaging in extensive reflection, devotion, prayer, and surrender to God and his presence. We are releasing our joys and complaints, while musing and studying upon a matter with him. We are absorbing, examining, exploring, studying and engaging with great thought and contemplation, where we become one in love, identity, and deed with what we are meditating about.

Soaking Meditation Activation:
1. Set an alarm for three minutes. Spend time cultivating the art of soaking by meditating upon the following scriptures.
2. Spend three minutes reflecting on each scripture before moving on to the next scripture.

Joshua 1:8 *This book of the law shall not depart out of thy mouth; but thou shalt meditate therein day and night, that thou mayest observe to do according to all that is written therein: for then thou shalt make thy way prosperous, and then thou shalt have good success.*

Psalms 19:14 *Let the words of my mouth, and the meditation of my heart, be acceptable in thy sight, O LORD, my strength, and my redeemer.*

Psalms 49:3 *My mouth shall speak of wisdom; and the meditation of my heart [shall be] of understanding.*

Psalms 63:6 *When I remember You on my bed, I meditate on You in the night watches,*

Psalms 104:34 *My meditation of him shall be sweet: I will be glad in the LORD.*

Psalms 119:11 *Thy word have I hid in mine heart, that I might not sin against thee.*

Psalms 119:15 *I will meditate in thy precepts, and have respect unto thy ways.*

Psalms 119:97-99 *O how love I thy law! it is my meditation all the day. Thou through thy commandments hast made me wiser than mine enemies: for they are ever with me. I have more understanding than all my teachers: for thy testimonies are my meditation.*

Proverbs 4:20-22 *My son, attend to my words; incline thine ear unto my sayings. Let them not depart from thine eyes; keep them in the midst of thine heart. For they are life unto those that find them, and health to all their flesh.*

Isaiah 26:3 *Thou wilt keep [him] in perfect peace, [whose] mind [is] stayed [on thee]: because he trusteth in thee.*

Philippians 4:8 *Finally, brethren, whatsoever things are true, whatsoever things [are] honest, whatsoever things [are] just, whatsoever things [are] pure, whatsoever things [are] lovely, whatsoever things [are] of good report; if [there be] any virtue, and if [there be] any praise, think on these things.*

SOAKING DELIGHTS

When we delight in someone or something, we spend time partaking and enjoying them or that thing. Delighting means we are taking our time to examine and consider every endeavor. We are savoring every moment while consuming all it entails.

> **Psalms 1:2** *But his delight is in the law of the LORD; and in his law doth he meditate day and night.*

> **Psalms 37:4-7** *Delight thyself also in the Lord; and he shall give thee the desires of thine heart. Commit thy way unto the Lord; trust also in him; and he shall bring it to pass. And he shall bring forth thy righteousness as the light, and thy judgment as the noonday. Rest in the Lord, and wait patiently for him: fret not thyself because of him who prospereth in his way, because of the man who bringeth wicked devices to pass.*

Rest in this passage of scripture is the Hebrew word *Damam* and means *"to be dumb, grow dumb, be struck dumb."* Your delight in God should be so astounding that it halts you, silences you, and strikes you to a place of muteness. Only learning to soak, while being still, standing in, tarrying, waiting, and longing in the presence of God can empower such a delight in you.

> **Psalms 94:19** *In the multitude of my thoughts within me thy comforts delight my soul.*

Soaking Delights Activation:
1. Set an alarm clock for ten minutes.
2. Spend ten minutes focusing on the love and goodness of God.
3. Examine and consider every aspect of God's love and goodness.

4. Allow yourself to delight in how it makes your heart feel and how it makes you feel about God.
5. Do not try to give back to him by thanking him, worshiping him, or praising him. Simply rest in the awareness of his goodness.
6. After ten minutes have passed, then begin to thank him, worship him, and praise him if you just cannot help yourself.

I Hide Myself Inside You Jesus!

I hide myself inside You Jesus, plunging urgently into the base of your harbor. Quieting myself inside You...My Rock. Invigorated rest that is sure to make me whole.

I hide myself inside You Jesus. All the good and comfort I know. Trusting the safety of Your tranquil peace...holy serenity. Divine respite that's sure to make me whole.

I hide myself inside You Jesus, mailing address Psalms 91...my own personal fortified stronghold. Living within the secret place of My Most High; Covenant refuge that's sure to make me whole.

I hide myself inside You Jesus...an embodied love with an ultimate eternal goal. True sacrificed expression establishing that I am yours always and forever. Jubilant devotion that's sure to make me whole.

I hide myself inside You Jesus!
Taquetta Baker

GOD'S INDWELLING

Dwelling means to live in God continually. A literal habitation has taken place where God lives in you and you live inside of him. You are one with God and are no longer the same as you take on the likeness of God and are transformed through the habitation of his glory.

God's Indwelling Activation:
1. Set an alarm for three minutes. Spend time cultivating your life as God's indwelling by meditating on each scripture for three minutes.
2. Ask God to give you revelations and visions of yourself living inside of him as you meditate on each scripture.
3. Spend three minutes reflecting on each scripture before moving on to the next scripture.
4. If God reveals you dwelling in a particular place with him, remain in that place for a while before going to the next scripture.
5. You want God's indwelling to become your daily habitat so complete this activation regularly with him.
6. Journal your experiences.

Genesis 5:24 Enoch walked with God; and he was not, for God took him.

Psalms 91:1 He that dwelleth in the secret place of the most High shall abide under the shadow of the Almighty.

John 3:6 That which is born of the flesh is flesh, and that which is born of the Spirit is spirit.

John 6:56 Whoever eats My flesh and drinks My blood remains in Me, and I in him.

John 10:28-29 And I give eternal life to them, and they will never perish; and no one will snatch them out of My hand. "My Father, who has given them to Me, is greater than all; and no one is able to snatch them out of the Father's hand.

John 14:23 *Jesus answered and said unto him, If a man love me, he will keep my words: and my Father will love him, and we will come unto him, and make our abode with him.*

John 15:4-5 *Abide in Me, and I in you. As the branch cannot bear fruit of itself unless it abides in the vine, so neither can you unless you abide in Me. "I am the vine, you are the branches; he who abides in Me and I in him, he bears much fruit, for apart from Me you can do nothing.*

John 15:7 *If you abide in Me, and My words abide in you, ask whatever you wish, and it will be done for you.*

1John 2:6 *the one who says he abides in Him ought himself to walk in the same manner as He walked.*

Ephesians 3:17-19 *so that Christ may dwell in your hearts through faith; and that you, being rooted and grounded in love, may be able to comprehend with all the saints what is the breadth and length and height and depth, and to know the love of Christ which surpasses knowledge, that you may be filled up to all the fullness of God.*

2Corinthians 5:17 *Therefore if anyone is in Christ, he is a new creature; the old things passed away; behold, new things have come.*

ABIDE IN CHRIST DECREE!

I am delivered because I am Deliverance.
I am healed because I am Healing.
I am boundary-less and limitless because I am Breakthrough.
I am saved because I am Salvation.
I am a living miracle because my daddy JESUS is The Miracle Worker.
I am miraculous because I am a Miracle Worker.
I perform miracles because I am Dunamis Power.
I am demon and stronghold free because I am Supreme Power Over Every Enemy.
I am victorious because I am Victory.
I am free because I am Holy Ghost Liberation.
I am sin free because I am the Habitation of God.
I am Holy fire because I am Baptized By Fire.
I am a glory carrier because I am Rivers Of Living Water.
I am healthy because I am Wellness.
I am complete because I am Wholeness.
I am blessed because I embody Blessings.
I am wealthy because I am Prosperity.
I am generous by I am Generosity.
I am a lender to nations because I am a Commandment Keeper.
I have the Spirit of excellence because I am Excellency.
I am unwavering faith because I am Radical Faith.
I am a mountain mover because I am Belief.
I am rooted and grounded because I am divine Foundation.
I am gifted because I have God's Substance.
I am the epitome of God because I am his Essence.
I lack nothing because I have God's Fullness.
I am integral because I am Godly Character.
I am the existence of God because I have his Nature.
I know truth because I am Truth.

I am uniquely me because I have God's Identity.
I am valiant because I am Strength.
I am fulfilled because I am Joy.
I love unconditionally because I am Love.
I work miracles because I am Compassion.
I am embracing because I am Gentleness.
I am loved because I am Kindness.
I am docile because I am Meekness.
I am humble because I am Humility.
I am balanced because I am Temperance.
I conquer tribulation because I am Peace.
I am patient because I am Patience.
I endure all because I am Long Suffering.
I have instruction because I am Counsel.
I have clarity because I am Understanding.
I am empowerment because I am Revelation.
I have information because I am Knowledge.
I have direction because I am Wisdom.
I have supernatural capability because I have Divine
Might.
I worship Jesus only because I am worship.
I honor Jesus because I am Reverence.
I serve Jesus because I am The Fear of The Lord.
I have destiny because I am Destiny.
I am marvelous because I am Magnificence.
I am successful because I am Greatness.
I create because I am Creation.
I recreate because I am like my Creator.
I transform because I am Transformation.
I establish the kingdom because I am Kingdom.
I advance the earth because I am a Trailblazer.
I am fruitful because I am Production.
I generate and regenerate because I am Reproduction.
I bring increase because I am Multiplication.
I have dominion in the earth because I am Subduer.
I govern the earth because I am a Dominion Heir and King.

I judge because I am Justice.
I birth and give life because I am Life.
I raise the dead because I am Resurrection.
I live forever because I am Eternal life.

LOST IN HIS PRESENCE!

I just want to be draped in Your awesome wonder, garnished in the beauty of Your wind of hush. Adorned in the ornaments of Your piety; elegance with a sacred touch...

I just want to be engrossed in Your heavenly manifestation with an intensity and depth beyond slain, doused in the power of Your royal brilliancy. Where my consciousness will no longer go in and out of Your sphere...Your rule, but live completely in Your divine monarchy....

I just want to be immersed in Your intangible glory whilst my physical self only feel and experience the warmth of Your eloquent rest; my existence shall appear numb....unresponsive, captivated in Your supernatural bliss.

I just want to be absorbed in the purity of Your angelic grander, mesmerized in Your staggering Shekinah cloud. My spirit shall achingly scream, "HOLY! HOLY! HOLY!" with vitality; spilling over that which fails to exude from my mouth!

I just want to be lost in Your splendor to a degree that there seems to be no return; a realm of unconsciousness where You and I are one.

I just want to be lost in Your presence!

By: Taquetta Baker

NUGGETS TO EFFECTIVE SOAKING

> Playing some soft instrumental music or even just resting in silence. I tend to do both. Sometimes, I will build a playlist that starts off with worship music that has words or scriptures to get my mind focused on Jesus then set the playlist to flow into some instrumental music so my mind can then focus on God and not be drawn to singing, worshipping, but just resting at the feet of Jesus.

> Silence! Siting in a quiet place in silence and just being with God. Not requiring anything of him or of yourself. Just being and seeing what comes of it. If nothing occurs, then be at peace that you just spent a moment with your God. The more you engage in silent soaking, the more you will be able to commune, hear, and obey God without gimmicks.

> Applying the blood of Jesus to your body, mind, spirit and soul, and asking for a cleansing of all sin and attachments that may hinder you from entering the presence of the Lord.

> Asking God's presence to come engulf you and resting while his presence consumes you.

> If I am still having trouble focusing, I will ask God for a picture of me being with him and I focus on that picture. My favorite picture is me lying across Jesus' feet. This is my favorite because I like to think if I am lying across his feet then he cannot go anywhere unless he kicks me off his feet, and Jesus is too loving to do that to me, right?

> When I soak, I tend to ask the Holy Spirit to lead the time, and whatever he places in my Spirit to focus on I focus on that. I will ask him what he desires and remain alert and focused on him or worship quietly until he speaks. Sometimes he will want me to lay prostrate, sometimes he will want me to kneel, and

sometimes he will want me to dance or worship with him, sometimes he will just want me to sit still and do or say nothing. If the Holy Spirit does not lead me in a focus then I try to spend time just resting and relaxing with Jesus. I try to remain conscious that sometimes Jesus just wants to rest and hang with me and we do not always need to be fixing or working on anything. And I do not always have to praise and worship or feel like I am working in prayer. At times, just like us, all God wants is to just be with us.

➤ If I do pray during this time, it is more of intimacy conversation. For example, sharing with God that I desire more of him and want to be closer to him. I may ask him questions about what he likes or what grieves him, what pleases him, what is important to him. I may ask him to give me more of his image, his glory, his healing power, and then I wait on him to manifest my request through his presence or voice.

➤ There are times when I may not feel Jesus' presence, but I have learned that this does not mean we are not communing. At times, we tend to gimmick God or attempt to get him to perform, and we use his presence as a measuring rod for knowing if he has engaged us or not. Some of the most profound revelations I have had from God have come when I have not felt his presence at all. And sometimes when soaking, I do not feel his presence and he may not speak a word, but there is simply a knowing in my Spirit that he is there and he is listening.

➤ I love to use scriptures when soaking or even to ask God for a scripture during my soaking time. The best scriptures for soaking are those that declare the dominion of Jesus, that declare his glory, and exalt him as the "Most High God." I also will ask Jesus to give me a scripture. Sometimes the scripture reveals how he feels about me, what he desires of me, or an answer or strategy to a situation I am praying for.

UNEXPLAINABLE DESIRE
FOR YOU JESUS!

My desire is unexplainable.
The words will not form in my mind.
I want to be inside your power.
Incognizant of kyros time.

In the midst of your holiness is where I want to be.
Not just an experience but a divine saturation of your heavenly.
One with you My Lord.
Purify my soul.
Every crevice consumed with you.
Hold me till I am whole.

Just have your way with me Lord
Manifest what my spirit cannot express.
I just want to be where ever you are.
Your heart is my one true quest.

My Desire Is Unexplainable For You Jesus!
By: Taquetta Baker

SOAKING VERSUS WITCHRAFT

Soaking is not yoga, witchcraft, astral projection, channeling, hypnosis or other worldly meditation methods that insight demons, idol gods, ancient powers, demonic energies or illegal supernatural practices. You are not pulling energies or strengths from idol gods, demonic forces, dead ancestors, or entertaining spirits and mysticisms unaware. Engaging in such tactics opens your body, soul, mind, spirit, and life to the possession of demonic spirits and occult activities, which are counterfeits to being consumed and governed by the only true savior - Jesus Christ and his Holy Spirit.

Many fear soaking is demonic because they do not want to risk engaging in the things I listed above. But you cannot resist engaging in another facet of prayer and communing with God for fear that you will entertain ungodly spirits and activities. If you are communing with Jesus Christ and the Holy Spirit then you should not encounter darkness unless he leads you into such realms for revelation, intercession, or warfare. And if Jesus led you, he will protect you and he will not allow you to be hurt, oppressed, or possessed.

Also, God will not lead you to absorb or partake of anything that is not his character and nature and that is of occult or witchcraft nature. Moreover, you should not be using spells, witchcraft, worldly or ungodly guided meditation, or demonic influences in effort to commune with God. Your soaking tactics should be focused on communing with God, allowing him to guide you in your interactions with him, while seeking to fill up and be transformed in his presence. You are simply spending time with God and allowing him to lead your time with him. You are tapping into your right to develop and cultivate a deeper intimate relationship with him and to be consumed by the benefits of his word and presence that makes you more like him. You may have supernatural experiences and encounters because you serve a supernatural God. However, soaking is about surrendering to intimate time with God and becoming one in communion, truth and identity with him.

Matthew 7:16 *Ye shall know them by their fruits. Do men gather grapes of thorns, or figs of thistles?*

Deuteronomy 18:10-12 *There shall not be found among you anyone who makes his son or his daughter pass through the fire, one who uses divination, one who practices witchcraft, or one who interprets omens, or a sorcerer, or one who casts a spell, or a medium, or a spiritist, or one who calls up the dead. "For whoever does these things is detestable to the LORD; and because of these detestable things the LORD your God will drive them out before you.*

Isaiah 8:19-20 *And when the people [instead of putting their trust in God] shall say to you, Consult for direction mediums and wizards who chirp and mutter, should not a people seek and consult their God? Should they consult the dead on behalf of the living? [Direct such people] to the teaching and to the testimony! If their teachings are not in accord with this word, it is surely because there is no dawn and no morning for them.*

1Timothy 4:1 *Now the Spirit speaketh expressly, that in the latter times some shall depart from the faith, giving heed to seducing spirits, and doctrines of devils.*

Ephesians 5:8-11 *For ye were sometimes darkness, but now are ye light in the Lord: walk as children of light: (For the fruit of the Spirit is in all goodness and righteousness and truth;) Proving what is acceptable unto the Lord. And have no fellowship with the unfruitful works of darkness, but rather reprove them.*

I want to take a moment to address yoga specifically because a lot of believers engage in yoga for meditation and exercise. Yoga is not a Christian practice. It is a witchcraft religion for the purposes of awakening and inviting the "Kundalini" spirit to live at the base of the spine in a person's body. I would encourage you to complete a google study on the Kundalini spirit and on yoga to learn more about what you are exposing your life to. Each yoga position is a demonic worship pose that offer sacrifices to the Kundalini spirit and other demonic entities attached to it. As you worship these deities through breathing techniques, meditation and exercise, you are relinquishing your body, soul, and spirit over to the Kundalini spirit and some 330 million Hindu gods - yes 330 million. Yoga is a Hindu practice and Hindus serve a god for each thing they desire to have occur in their lives. They may have:

- A god for finances
- A god for health
- A god for success
- A god for peace
- A god for love
- A god for protection
- A god for energy
- And on and on

Though you may experience peace, calming effect, supernatural strength, life success, and wellness through yoga, it is through demonic deities and witchcraft that is invading your body, mind, soul, and spirit, creating an illusion of God's true peace, will and purpose for your life. Yet, you are sacrificing your life to idols. As you are learning their techniques and poses, you are allowing that idol god and energy to come into that area of your life and govern it. Your natural strength and ability to complete the yoga poses with comfort and fortitude is a spiritual reflection of the impact and influence that god has over your life.

> **Romans 12:1-2 (*The Amplified Version*)** *I APPEAL to you therefore, brethren, and beg of you in view of [all] the mercies of God, to make a decisive dedication of your bodies [presenting all your members and faculties] as a living sacrifice, holy (devoted, consecrated) and well pleasing to God, which is your reasonable (rational, intelligent) service and spiritual worship. Do not be conformed to this world (this age), [fashioned after and adapted to its external, superficial customs], but be transformed (changed) by the [entire] renewal of your mind [by its new ideals and its new attitude], so that you may prove [for yourselves] what is the good and acceptable and perfect will of God, even the thing which is good and acceptable and perfect [in His sight for you].*

> **Acts 15:29 (*The Amplified Version*)** *That you abstain from what has been sacrificed to idols and from [tasting] blood and from [eating the meat of animals] that have been strangled and from sexual impurity. If you keep yourselves from these things, you will do well. Farewell [be strong]!*

> **John 14:27** *Peace I leave with you, my peace I give unto you: not as the world giveth, give I unto you. Let not your heart be troubled, neither let it be afraid.*

At the time you are experiencing relief, it does not appear that yoga is releasing trouble into your life. But the enemy is a deceiver who comes as light.

2Corinthians 11:14 (*New International Version*) *And no wonder, for Satan himself masquerades as an angel of light.*

Even if you contend that when you are doing yoga you are meditating on God, there is no giving way to the fact that the techniques are witchcraft and demonically rooted and focused. God is not receiving them as sacrifices to him. And he is not engaging you when you are participating in demonic activities, unless it is to convict your heart so that you will know it is not of him. Most likely, if you are meditating on Jesus or trying to engage the Holy Spirit while doing yoga, and do not have an inkling that your actions are wrong, you are engaging a false Jesus or false Holy Spirit. You are encountering pretender deities that are making you think yoga is okay and God is pleased with your actions.

> **Zechariah 10:2** *For the teraphim speak iniquity, And the diviners see lying visions And tell false dreams; They comfort in vain Therefore the people wander like sheep, They are afflicted, because there is no shepherd.*

Moreover, the breathing techniques in yoga is *pranayama* breathing. *Prana* is the Hindu word for life force, which is the same concept as the word tai chi in some martial arts. *Tai Chi* relies on the manipulation of mythical energies to draw power and ability for completing different martial art movements. As you are utilizing the breathing techniques you are participating in what yoga titles "*an emptying of the mind,*" which can cause a person to leave their body and engage in astral projection. Astral projection is a voluntary out of body experience. It is illegal without the leading of the Holy Spirit and is deemed as witchcraft when done without the direction of God.

Astral Projection led by God
- 2Corinthians 12-1-4
- Ezekiel 8:3
- Ezekiel 37:1-14
- Acts 8:39
- Acts 10:10
- Revelations 4:1-2

When you are not led by God, you are trespassing in the spirit realm and yielding to divination and witchcraft.

> *Deuteronomy 18:10-12 There shall not be found among you anyone who makes his son or his daughter pass through the fire, one who uses divination, one who practices witchcraft, or one who interprets omens, or a sorcerer, or one who casts a spell, or a medium, or a spiritist, or one who calls up the dead. "For whoever does these things is detestable to the LORD; and because of these detestable things the LORD your God will drive them out before you.*

As believers, we should be cleansing our minds of anything that is not like God, we however, should not be leaving our bodies to do so. Per **Roman 12:2**, we should be seeking transformation through the renewing our minds which can be done through soaking prayer. We should not be wandering around or exposing ourselves to spiritual realms without the leading of the Holy Spirit. To do so exposes us to demonic oppression and infestation. And even for those who say they do not astral project, *Tai Chi* is still inviting demonic spiritual energies into your life which is witchcraft and divination.

FALL ON ME!

By: Taquetta Baker

With an urgent craving I bellow in a plea,
"Let Your manifested glory fall in a splash immersing me with
tranquility!"
Fall on me Lord! Fall on me!

For I desire us to be as one, worshipping You with a shhhhhhhh.
Awed by Your presence that shall invade me in a stir.
Fall on me Lord! Fall!
As heavenly mirth; Fall! Fall Lord!
Fall in a hush!

Decrease me Lord and let Your presence increase in me.
Do a Holy Ghost take over in my life…Fall Lord! Fall!
Captivate my soul while setting my being free.

And in a twinkling of an eye a cloud of midst fills
the temple with surpassing peace,
My spirit yearningly marvels, Yes Lord!
Yes! Fall! Fall! Fall on me!

As the color of Amber, vivid orange fiery red ironclads
exude from the drizzling cloud. Brightness of rays beam with
great power and glory purifies the atmosphere, purging the entire
temple
with grace and mercy, enhancing its beauty with an angelic clout.
Fall My Lord! Fall! Fall on me!

Let Your manifested glory Fall! I want more of You Lord!
More! More! Fall on me!

His glory reigns in a drenching, it begins to be unbearable.
Humanly too much! Buckling…dropping me to my knees.
In a reverence at His mystifying touch.

I open my mouth to glorify Him but nothing comes out.
I am falling He says….Falling!
Granting the request of my beautiful child.

And we are as one in the radiance of His glory cloud.
His manifested presence falls.
Filling my famine in an overflowing flood

FALL OH LORD! FALL! FALL ON ME!

References

Scripture references are from:
www.biblegateway.com
www.blueletterbible.com
www.crosswalk.com
www.Wikipedia.com

Definitions are quoted from:
www.answers.com
www.m-w.com
www.dictionary.com

Book photo of Taquetta was taken by Tashema Davis.
Book Cover was designed by Reenita Keys.
Connect with them via Facebook.

Kingdom Shifters Books & Apparel
Available at Kingdomshifters.com

BOOKS FOR EVERYONE

Healing The Wounded Leader

Kingdom Shifters Decree That Thang

There Is An App For That

Kingdom Watchman Builder On the Wall

Embodiment Of A Kingdom Watchman

Dismantling Homosexuality Handbook

Feasting In His Presence

Releasing The Vision

Kingdom Heirs Decree That Thing

Let There Be Sight

Atmosphere Changers (Weaponry

BOOKS FOR DANCERS
Dancers! Dancers! Decree That Thang
Spirits That Attack Dance Ministers & Ministries

TEE SHIRTS

Kingdom Shifters Tee Shirt
Releasing The Vision Tee Shirt
Stand in Position Tee Shirt
My God Rules Like A Boss Tee Shirt

Let The Fruit Speak Tee Shirt
Kingdom Perspective Tee Shirt
No Defense Tee Shirt
Destiny Blueprint Tee Shirt

CD'S
Decree That Thing CD
Kingdom Heirs Decree That Thing CD
Teachings & Worship CD's